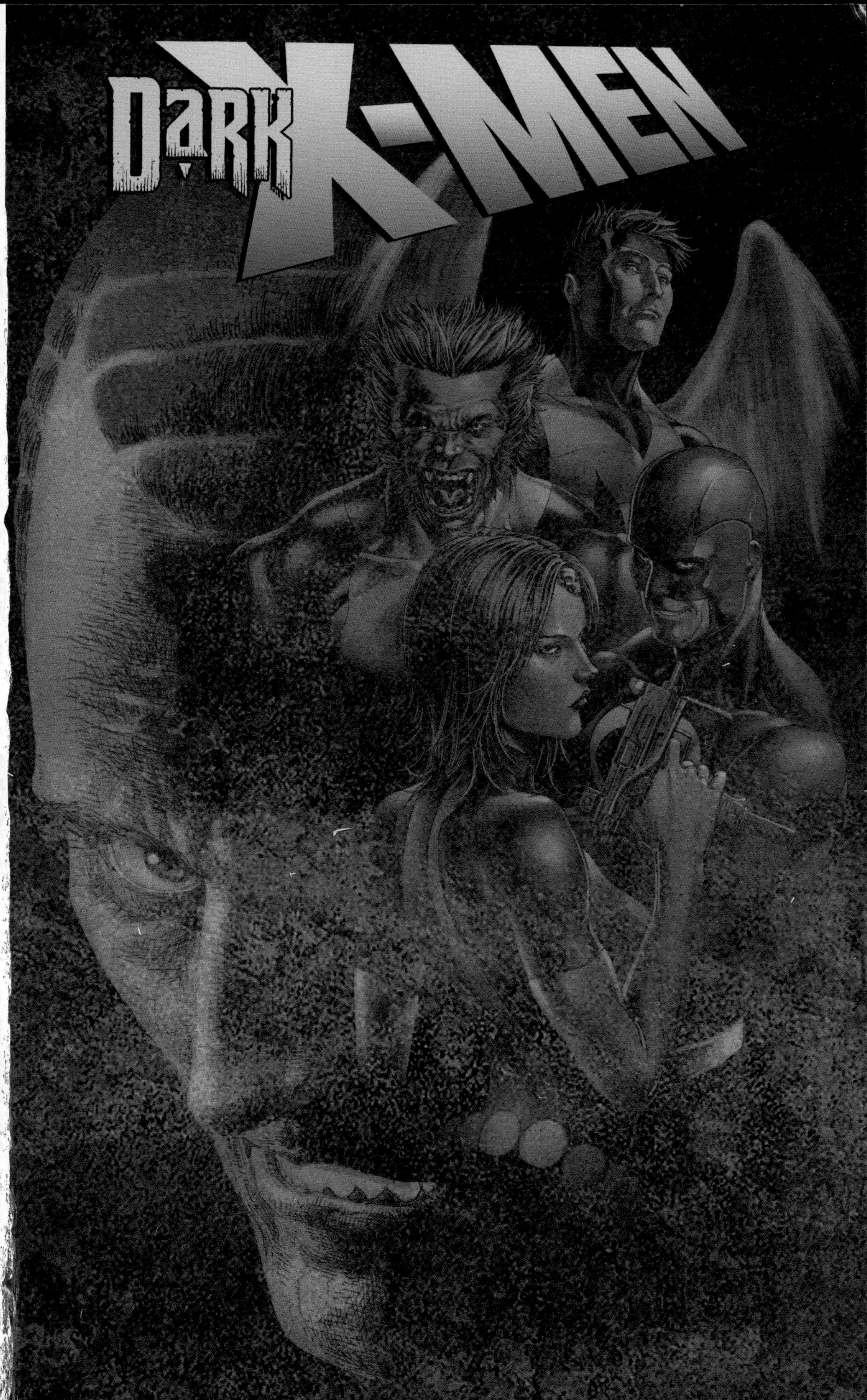
DARK X-MEN

DARK X-MEN

Collection Editor
JENNIFER GRÜNWALD

Assistant Editor
ALEX STARBUCK

Associate Editor
JOHN DENNING

Editor, Special Projects
MARK D. BEAZLEY

Senior Editor, Special Projects
JEFF YOUNGQUIST

Senior Vice President of Sales
DAVID GABRIEL

Book Design
JEFF POWELL

Editor in Chief
JOE QUESADA

Publisher
DAN BUCKLEY

Executive Producer
ALAN FINE

DARK X-MEN. Contains material originally published in magazine form as DARK X-MEN #1-5. First printing 2010. ISBN# 978-0-7851-4526-4. Published by MARVEL WORLDWIDE, INC., a subsidiary of MARVEL ENTERTAINMENT, LLC. OFFICE OF PUBLICATION: 417 5th Avenue, New York, NY 10016. Copyright © 2009 and 2010 Marvel Characters, Inc. All rights reserved. $19.99 per copy in the U.S. (GST #R127032852); Canadian Agreement #40668537. All characters featured in this issue and the distinctive names and likenesses thereof, and all related indicia are trademarks of Marvel Characters, Inc. No similarity between any of the names, characters, persons, and/or institutions in this magazine with those of any living or dead person or institution is intended, and any such similarity which may exist is purely coincidental. **Printed in the U.S.A.** ALAN FINE, EVP - Office of the President, Marvel Worldwide, Inc. and EVP & CMO Marvel Characters B.V.; DAN BUCKLEY, Chief Executive Officer and Publisher - Print, Animation & Digital Media; JIM SOKOLOWSKI, Chief Operating Officer; DAVID GABRIEL, SVP of Publishing Sales & Circulation; DAVID BOGART, SVP of Business Affairs & Talent Management; MICHAEL PASCIULLO, VP Merchandising & Communications; JIM O'KEEFE, VP of Operations & Logistics; DAN CARR, Executive Director of Publishing Technology; JUSTIN F. GABRIE, Director of Publishing & Editorial Operations; SUSAN CRESPI, Editorial Operations Manager; ALEX MORALES, Publishing Operations Manager; STAN LEE, Chairman Emeritus. For information regarding advertising in Marvel Comics or on Marvel.com, please contact Ron Stern, VP of Business Development, at rstern@marvel.com. For Marvel subscription inquiries, please call 800-217-9158. **Manufactured between 3/22/10 and 4/21/10 by R.R. DONNELLEY, INC., SALEM, VA, USA.**

10 9 8 7 6 5 4 3 2 1

WRITER
PAUL CORNELL

PENCILER
LEONARD KIRK

INKERS
**JAY LEISTEN &
LEONARD KIRK**
(ISSUES #4-5)

COLORIST
BRIAN REBER

LETTERER
ROB STEEN

COVER ARTISTS
SIMONE BIANCHI WITH
SIMONE PERUZZI
(ISSUES #1-3)
MIKE CHOI & SONIA OBACK
(ISSUE #4)
AND **GIUSEPPE CAMUNCOLI
& MORRY HOLLOWELL**
(ISSUE #5)

ASSOCIATE EDITOR
DANIEL KETCHUM

EDITOR
NICK LOWE

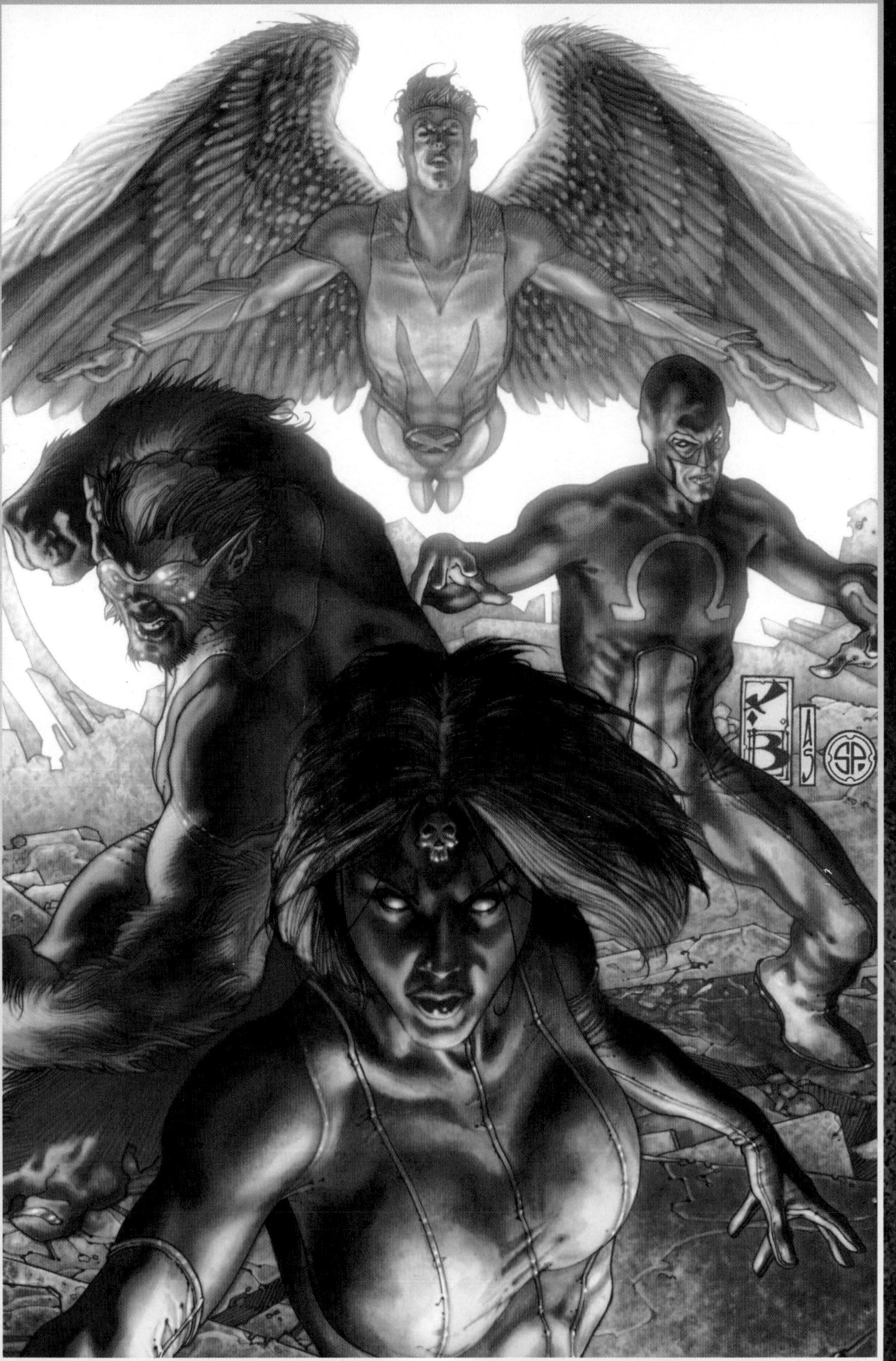

1

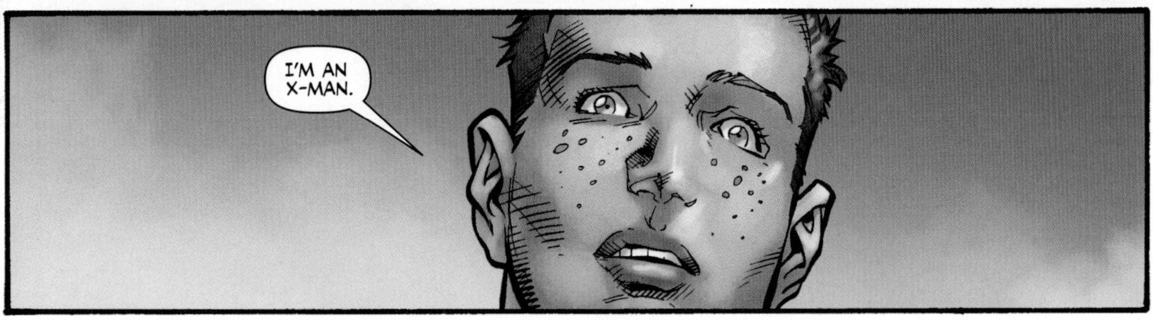
I'M AN X-MAN.

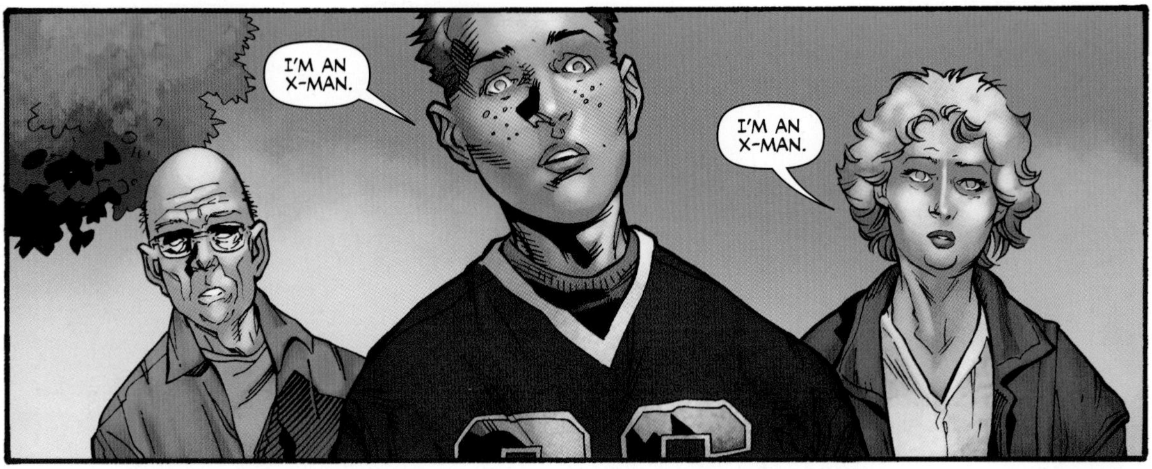
I'M AN X-MAN.
I'M AN X-MAN.

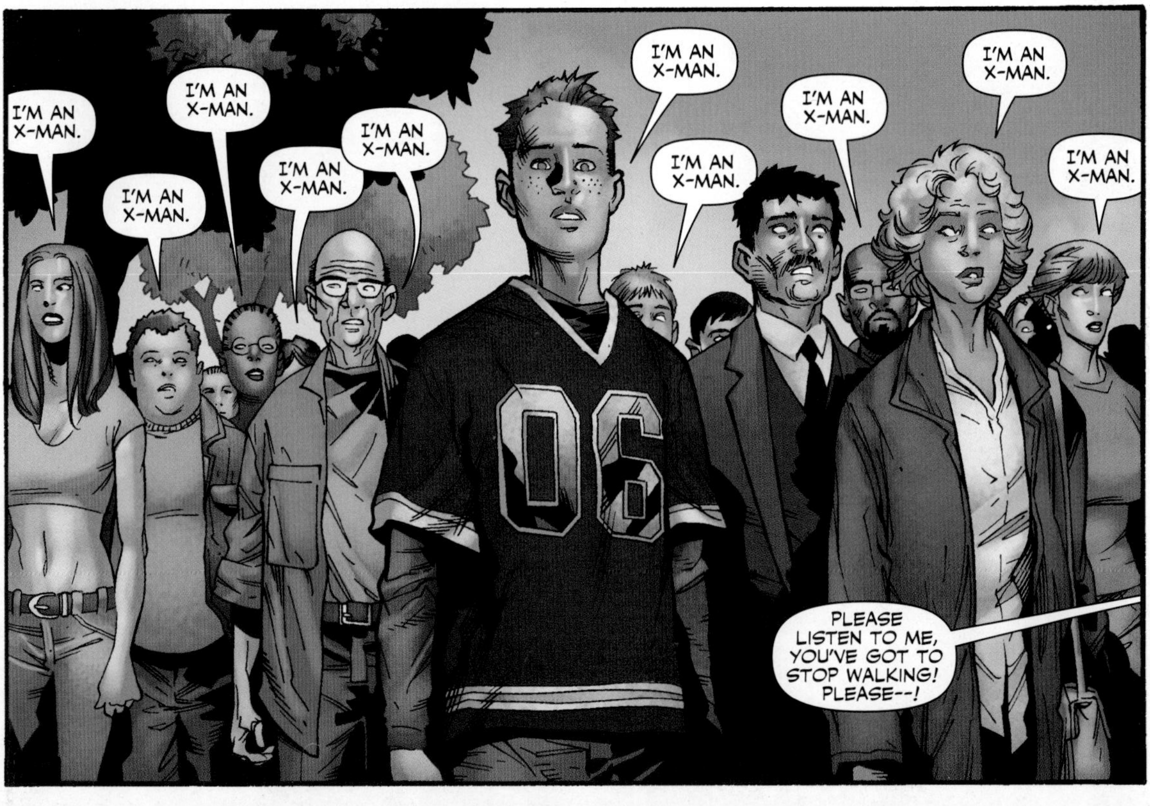
I'M AN X-MAN.
I'M AN X-MAN.
I'M AN X-MAN.
I'M AN X-MAN.
I'M AN X-MAN.
I'M AN X-MAN.
I'M AN X-MAN.
I'M AN X-MAN.
I'M AN X-MAN.
I'M AN X-MAN.
PLEASE LISTEN TO ME, YOU'VE GOT TO STOP WALKING! PLEASE--!

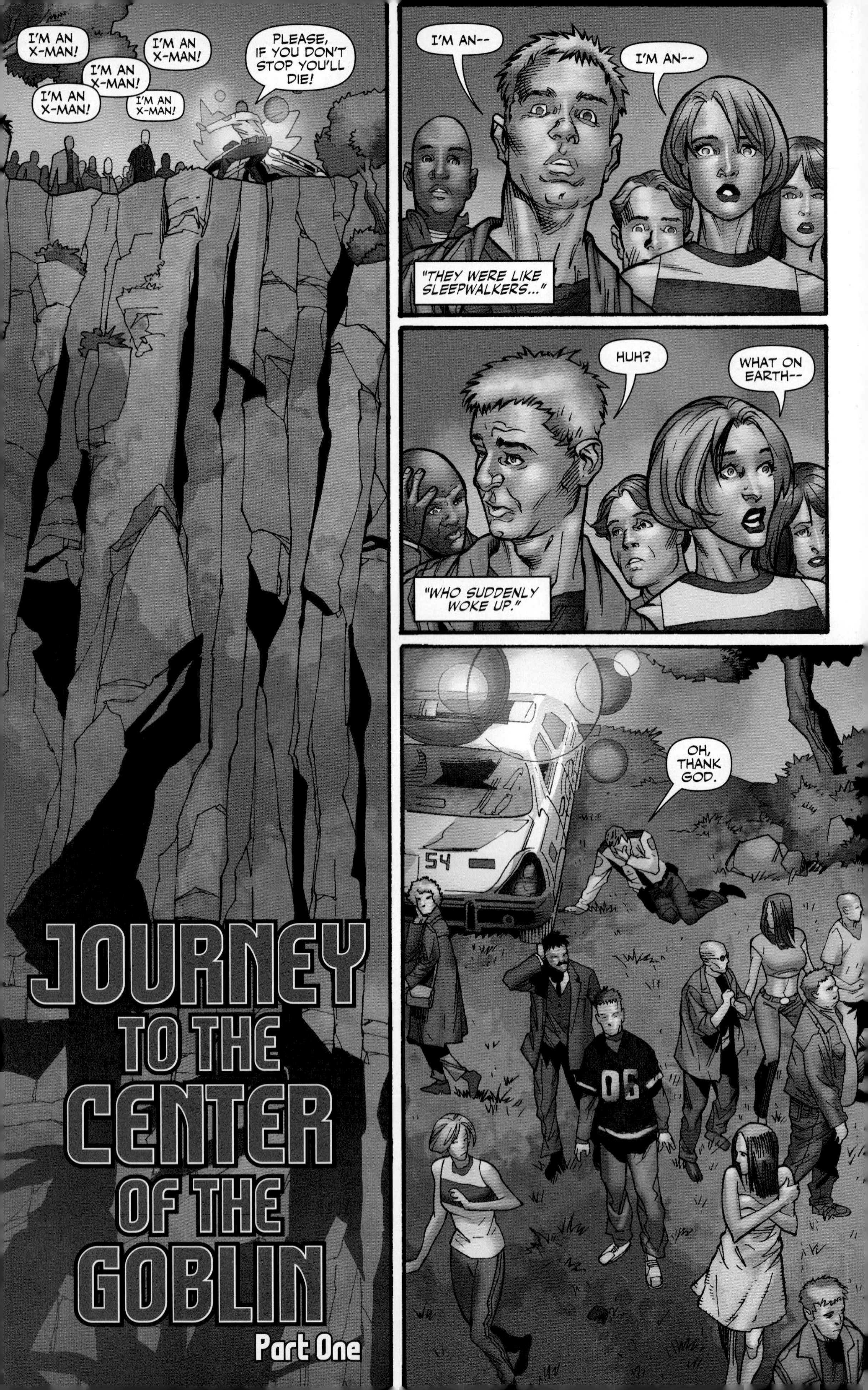
I'M AN X-MAN!
I'M AN X-MAN!
I'M AN X-MAN!
I'M AN X-MAN!
I'M AN X-MAN!
PLEASE, IF YOU DON'T STOP YOU'LL DIE!
JOURNEY TO THE CENTER OF THE GOBLIN
Part One
I'M AN--
I'M AN--
"THEY WERE LIKE SLEEPWALKERS..."
HUH?
WHAT ON EARTH--
"WHO SUDDENLY WOKE UP."
OH, THANK GOD.
54
06

Following the failed Skrull invasion of Earth, Norman
Osborn became the Director of the national peacekeeping
organization H.A.M.M.E.R. and leader of the Avengers.
Finding himself in need of a means for policing America's
mutant population during riots in San Francisco that
involved the X-Men, Norman recruited his own team of
X-Men to be the face of law and order for mutantkind...

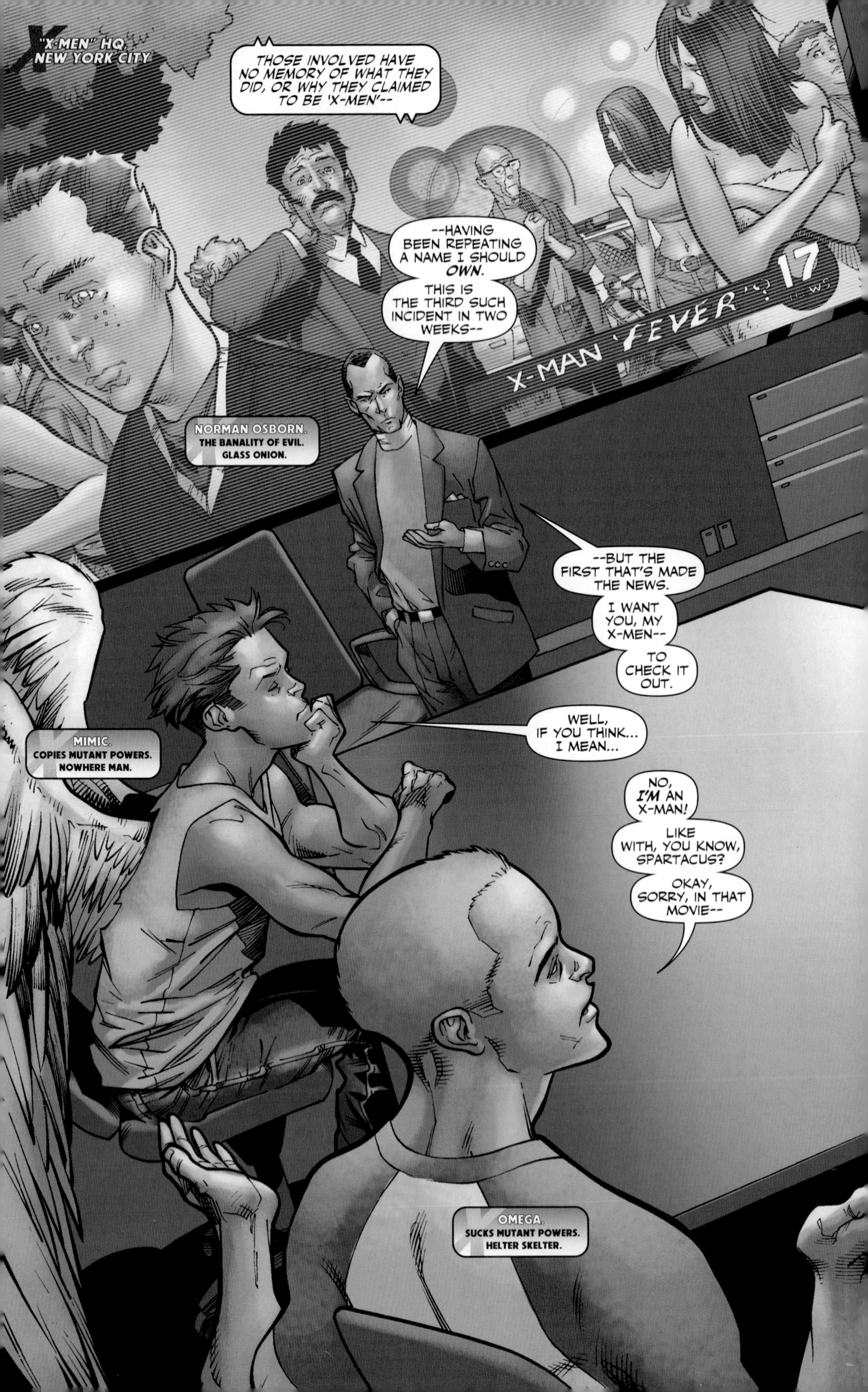

"X-MEN" HQ, NEW YORK CITY
THOSE INVOLVED HAVE NO MEMORY OF WHAT THEY DID, OR WHY THEY CLAIMED TO BE 'X-MEN'--
--HAVING BEEN REPEATING A NAME I SHOULD OWN.
THIS IS THE THIRD SUCH INCIDENT IN TWO WEEKS--
X-MAN 'FEVER'?
17
NORMAN OSBORN. THE BANALITY OF EVIL. GLASS ONION.
--BUT THE FIRST THAT'S MADE THE NEWS.
I WANT YOU, MY X-MEN--
TO CHECK IT OUT.
WELL, IF YOU THINK... I MEAN...
MIMIC. COPIES MUTANT POWERS. NOWHERE MAN.
NO, I'M AN X-MAN!
LIKE WITH, YOU KNOW, SPARTACUS?
OKAY, SORRY, IN THAT MOVIE--
OMEGA. SUCKS MUTANT POWERS. HELTER SKELTER.

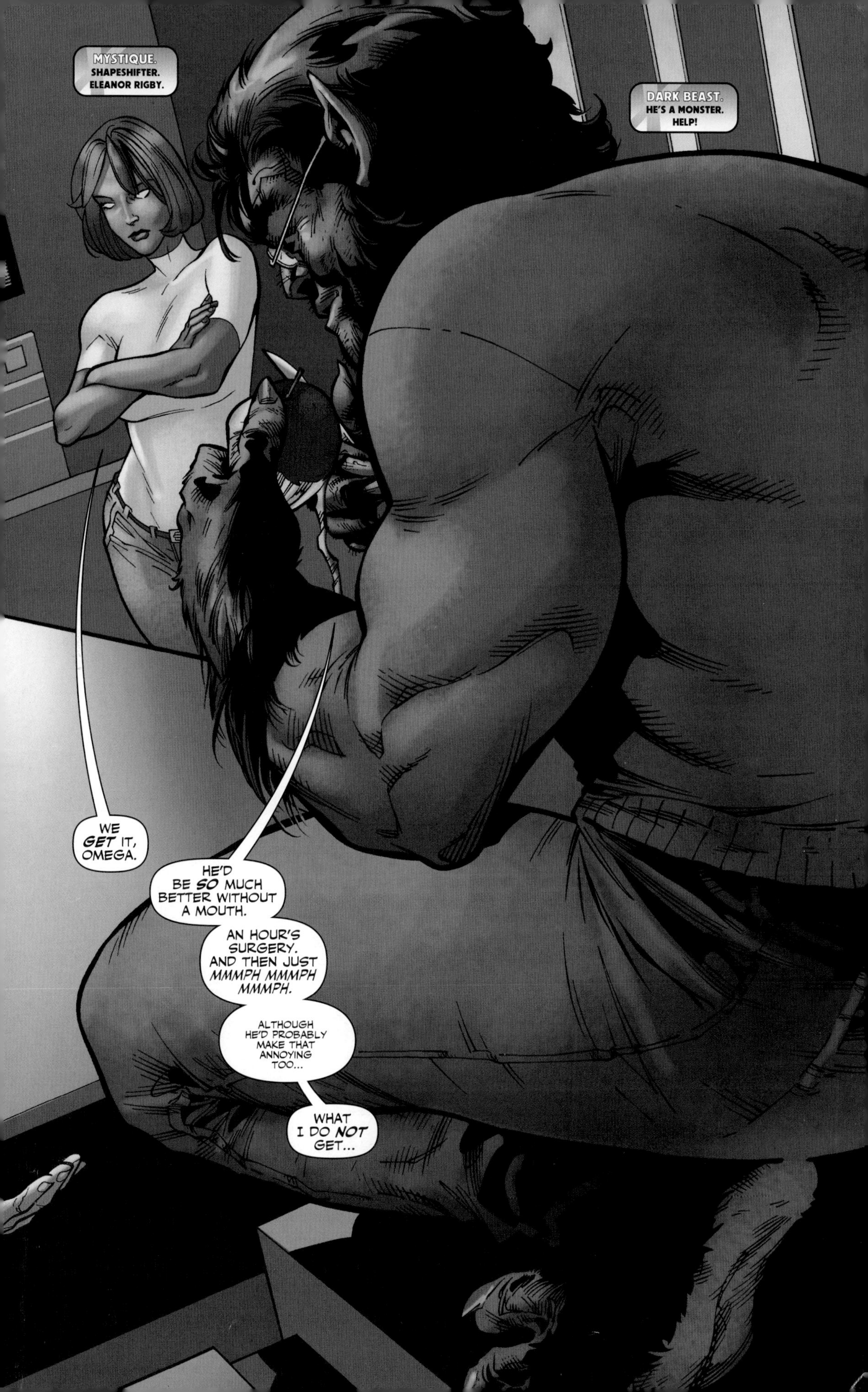

MYSTIQUE.
SHAPESHIFTER.
ELEANOR RIGBY.
DARK BEAST.
HE'S A MONSTER.
HELP!
WE GET IT, OMEGA.
HE'D BE SO MUCH BETTER WITHOUT A MOUTH.
AN HOUR'S SURGERY. AND THEN JUST MMMPH MMMPH MMMPH.
ALTHOUGH HE'D PROBABLY MAKE THAT ANNOYING TOO...
WHAT I DO NOT GET...

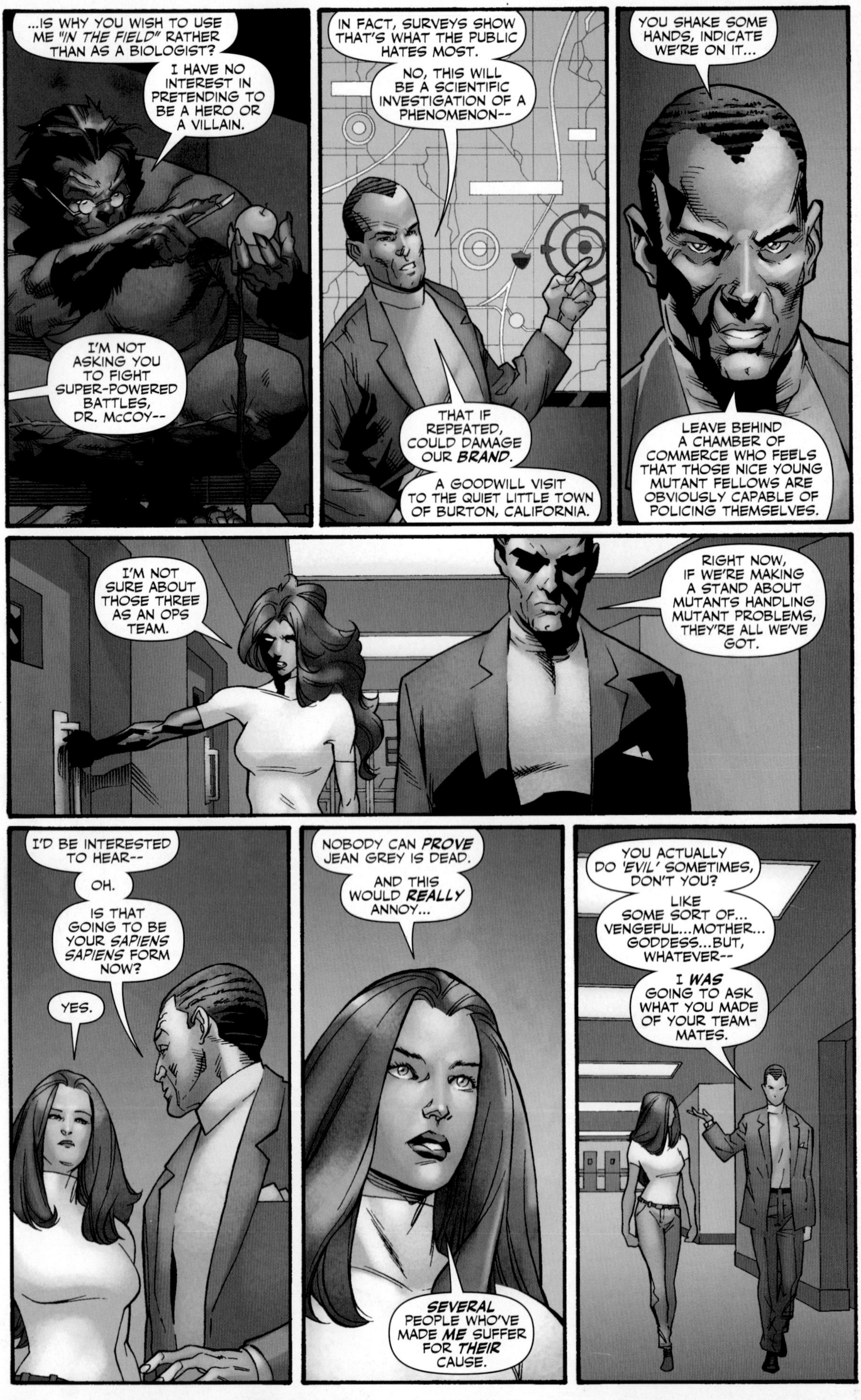
...IS WHY YOU WISH TO USE ME "IN THE FIELD" RATHER THAN AS A BIOLOGIST?
I HAVE NO INTEREST IN PRETENDING TO BE A HERO OR A VILLAIN.
I'M NOT ASKING YOU TO FIGHT SUPER-POWERED BATTLES, DR. McCOY--
IN FACT, SURVEYS SHOW THAT'S WHAT THE PUBLIC HATES MOST.
NO, THIS WILL BE A SCIENTIFIC INVESTIGATION OF A PHENOMENON--
THAT IF REPEATED, COULD DAMAGE OUR BRAND.
A GOODWILL VISIT TO THE QUIET LITTLE TOWN OF BURTON, CALIFORNIA.
YOU SHAKE SOME HANDS, INDICATE WE'RE ON IT...
LEAVE BEHIND A CHAMBER OF COMMERCE WHO FEELS THAT THOSE NICE YOUNG MUTANT FELLOWS ARE OBVIOUSLY CAPABLE OF POLICING THEMSELVES.
I'M NOT SURE ABOUT THOSE THREE AS AN OPS TEAM.
RIGHT NOW, IF WE'RE MAKING A STAND ABOUT MUTANTS HANDLING MUTANT PROBLEMS, THEY'RE ALL WE'VE GOT.
I'D BE INTERESTED TO HEAR--
OH.
IS THAT GOING TO BE YOUR SAPIENS SAPIENS FORM NOW?
YES.
NOBODY CAN PROVE JEAN GREY IS DEAD.
AND THIS WOULD REALLY ANNOY...
SEVERAL PEOPLE WHO'VE MADE ME SUFFER FOR THEIR CAUSE.
YOU ACTUALLY DO 'EVIL' SOMETIMES, DON'T YOU?
LIKE SOME SORT OF... VENGEFUL...MOTHER... GODDESS...BUT, WHATEVER--
I WAS GOING TO ASK WHAT YOU MADE OF YOUR TEAM-MATES.

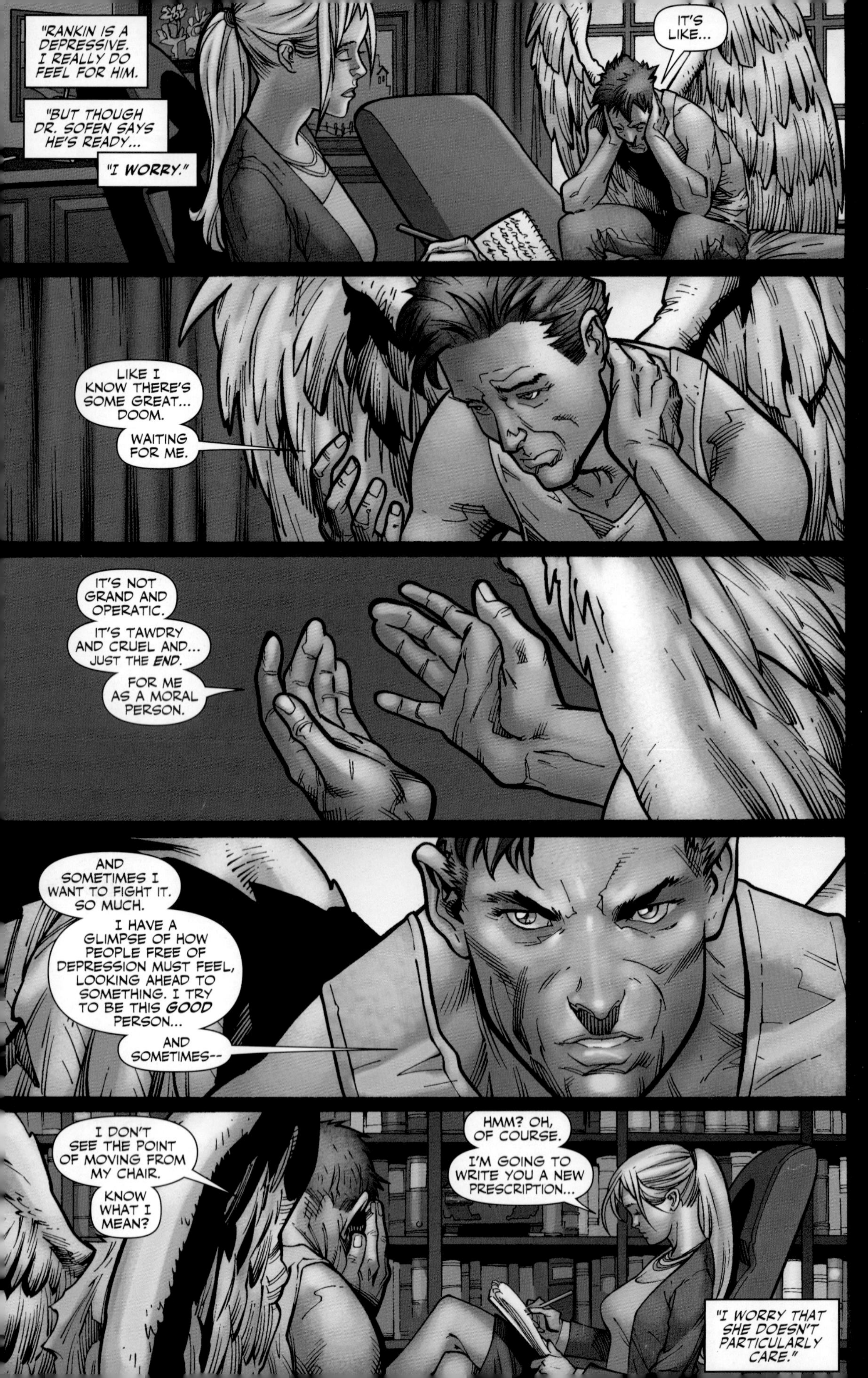
"RANKIN IS A DEPRESSIVE. I REALLY DO FEEL FOR HIM.
"BUT THOUGH DR. SOFEN SAYS HE'S READY...
"I WORRY."
IT'S LIKE...
LIKE I KNOW THERE'S SOME GREAT... DOOM.
WAITING FOR ME.
IT'S NOT GRAND AND OPERATIC.
IT'S TAWDRY AND CRUEL AND... JUST THE END.
FOR ME AS A MORAL PERSON.
AND SOMETIMES I WANT TO FIGHT IT. SO MUCH.
I HAVE A GLIMPSE OF HOW PEOPLE FREE OF DEPRESSION MUST FEEL, LOOKING AHEAD TO SOMETHING. I TRY TO BE THIS GOOD PERSON...
AND SOMETIMES--
I DON'T SEE THE POINT OF MOVING FROM MY CHAIR.
KNOW WHAT I MEAN?
HMM? OH, OF COURSE.
I'M GOING TO WRITE YOU A NEW PRESCRIPTION...
"I WORRY THAT SHE DOESN'T PARTICULARLY CARE."

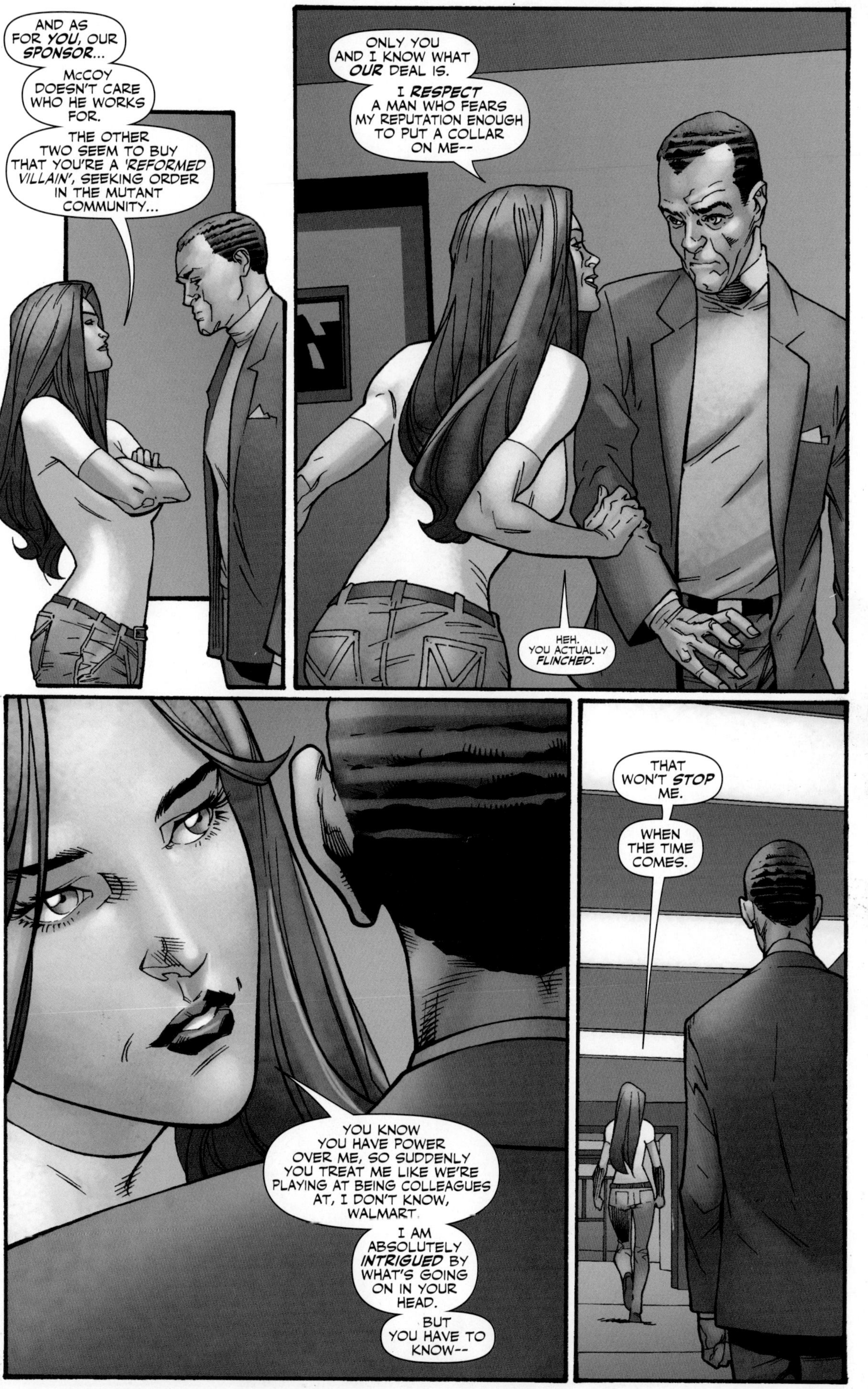
AND AS FOR YOU, OUR SPONSOR...
McCOY DOESN'T CARE WHO HE WORKS FOR.
THE OTHER TWO SEEM TO BUY THAT YOU'RE A 'REFORMED VILLAIN', SEEKING ORDER IN THE MUTANT COMMUNITY...
ONLY YOU AND I KNOW WHAT OUR DEAL IS.
I RESPECT A MAN WHO FEARS MY REPUTATION ENOUGH TO PUT A COLLAR ON ME--
HEH. YOU ACTUALLY FLINCHED.
YOU KNOW YOU HAVE POWER OVER ME, SO SUDDENLY YOU TREAT ME LIKE WE'RE PLAYING AT BEING COLLEAGUES AT, I DON'T KNOW, WALMART.
I AM ABSOLUTELY INTRIGUED BY WHAT'S GOING ON IN YOUR HEAD.
BUT YOU HAVE TO KNOW--
THAT WON'T STOP ME.
WHEN THE TIME COMES.

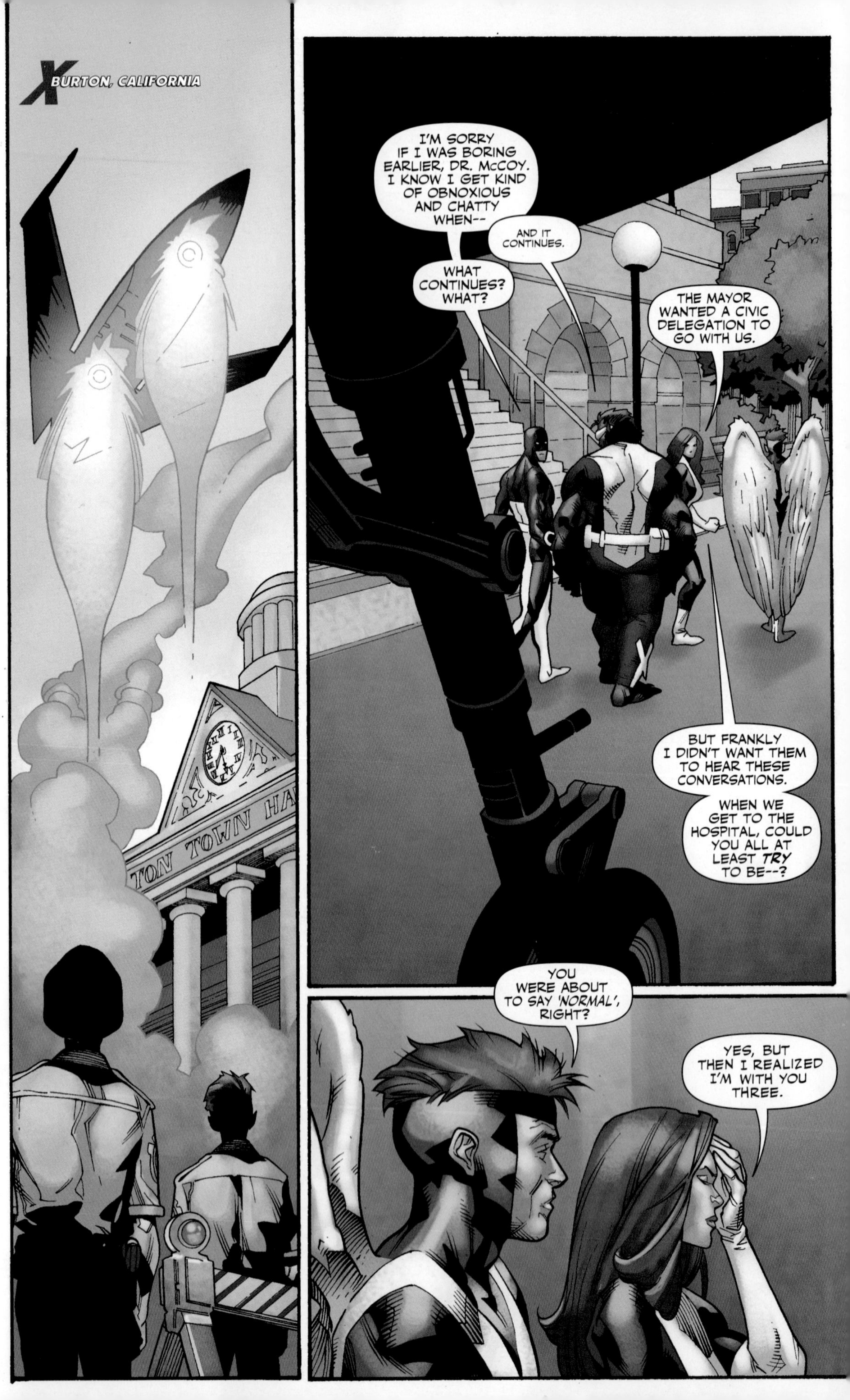
BURTON, CALIFORNIA
TON TOWN HA
I'M SORRY IF I WAS BORING EARLIER, DR. McCOY. I KNOW I GET KIND OF OBNOXIOUS AND CHATTY WHEN--
AND IT CONTINUES.
WHAT CONTINUES? WHAT?
THE MAYOR WANTED A CIVIC DELEGATION TO GO WITH US.
BUT FRANKLY I DIDN'T WANT THEM TO HEAR THESE CONVERSATIONS.
WHEN WE GET TO THE HOSPITAL, COULD YOU ALL AT LEAST *TRY* TO BE--?
YOU WERE ABOUT TO SAY *'NORMAL'*, RIGHT?
YES, BUT THEN I REALIZED I'M WITH YOU THREE.

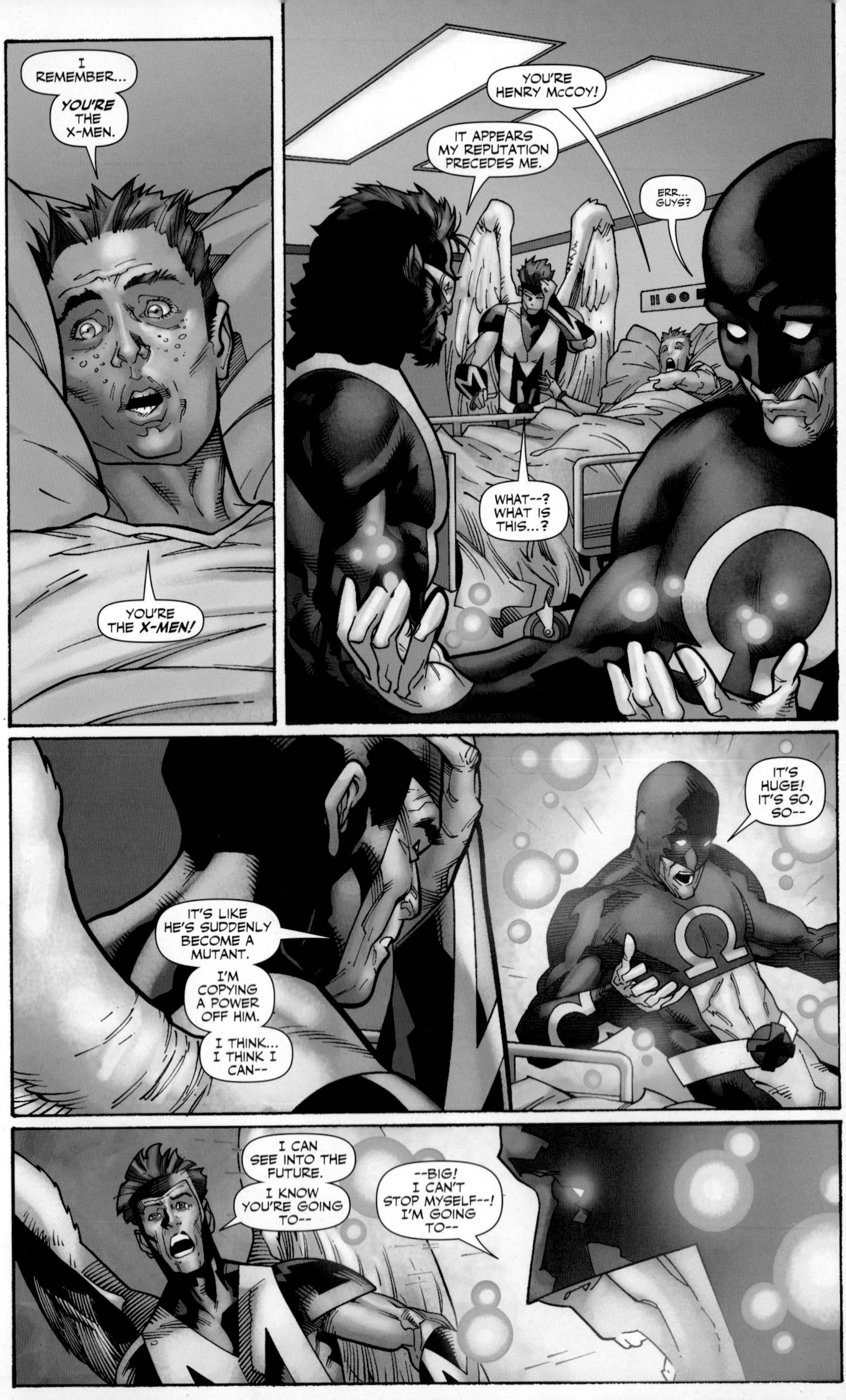
I REMEMBER...
YOU'RE THE X-MEN.
YOU'RE THE X-MEN!
YOU'RE HENRY McCOY!
IT APPEARS MY REPUTATION PRECEDES ME.
ERR... GUYS?
WHAT--? WHAT IS THIS...?
IT'S HUGE! IT'S SO, SO--
IT'S LIKE HE'S SUDDENLY BECOME A MUTANT.
I'M COPYING A POWER OFF HIM.
I THINK... I THINK I CAN--
I CAN SEE INTO THE FUTURE.
I KNOW YOU'RE GOING TO--
--BIG! I CAN'T STOP MYSELF--! I'M GOING TO--

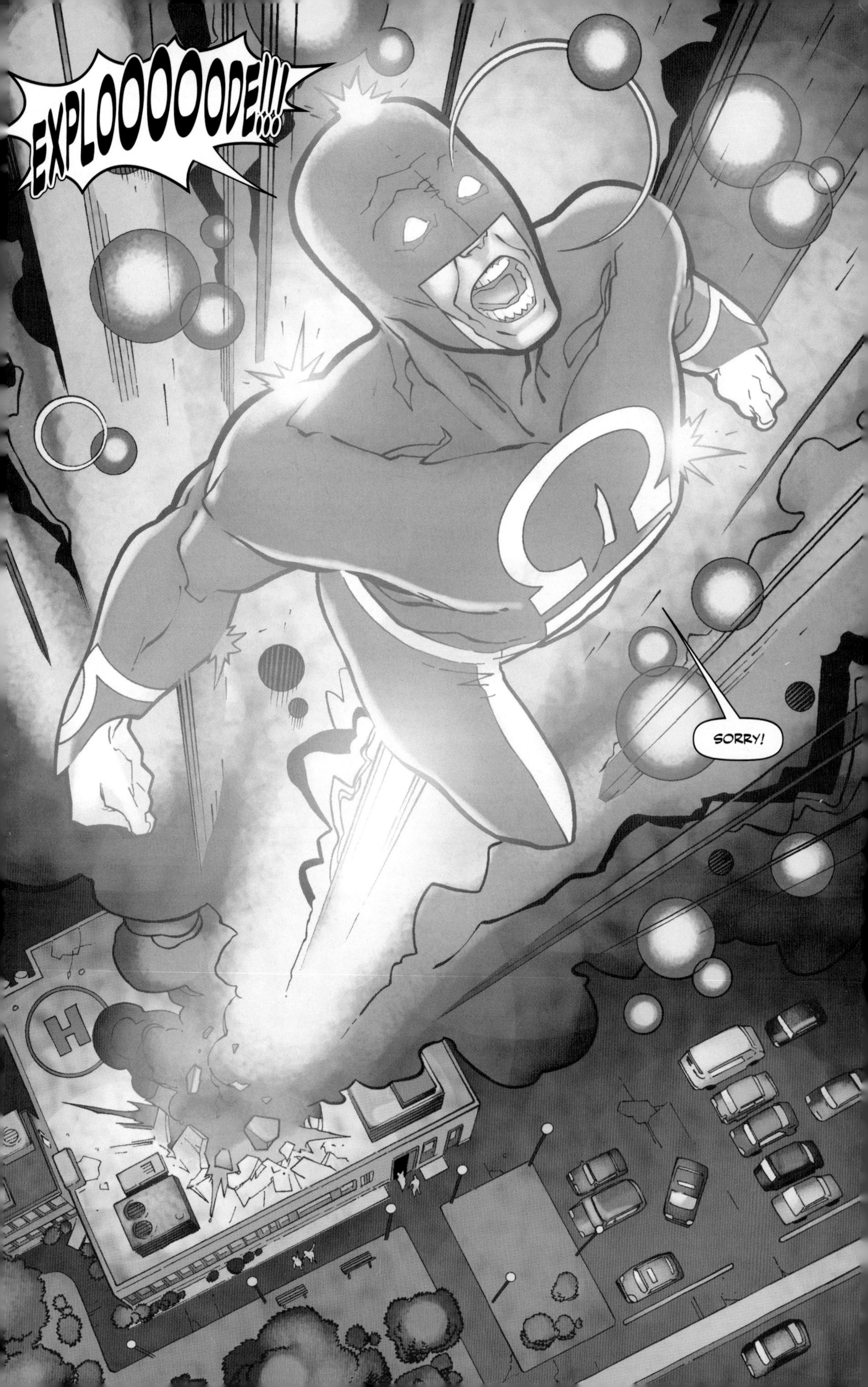
EXPLOOOOODE!!!
SORRY!

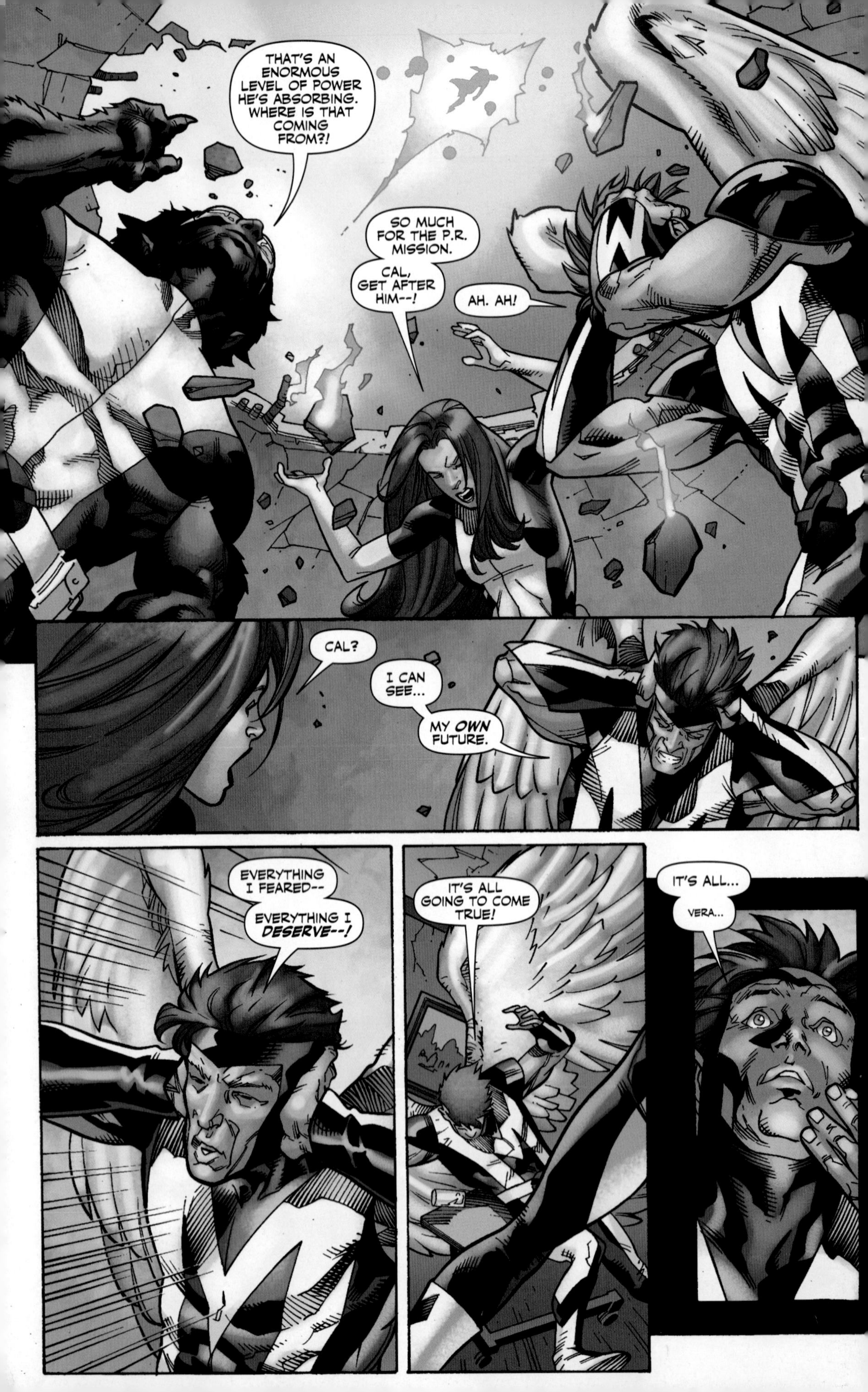
THAT'S AN ENORMOUS LEVEL OF POWER HE'S ABSORBING. WHERE IS THAT COMING FROM?!
SO MUCH FOR THE P.R. MISSION.
CAL, GET AFTER HIM--!
AH. AH!
CAL?
I CAN SEE...
MY OWN FUTURE.
EVERYTHING I FEARED--
EVERYTHING I DESERVE--!
IT'S ALL GOING TO COME TRUE!
IT'S ALL...
VERA...

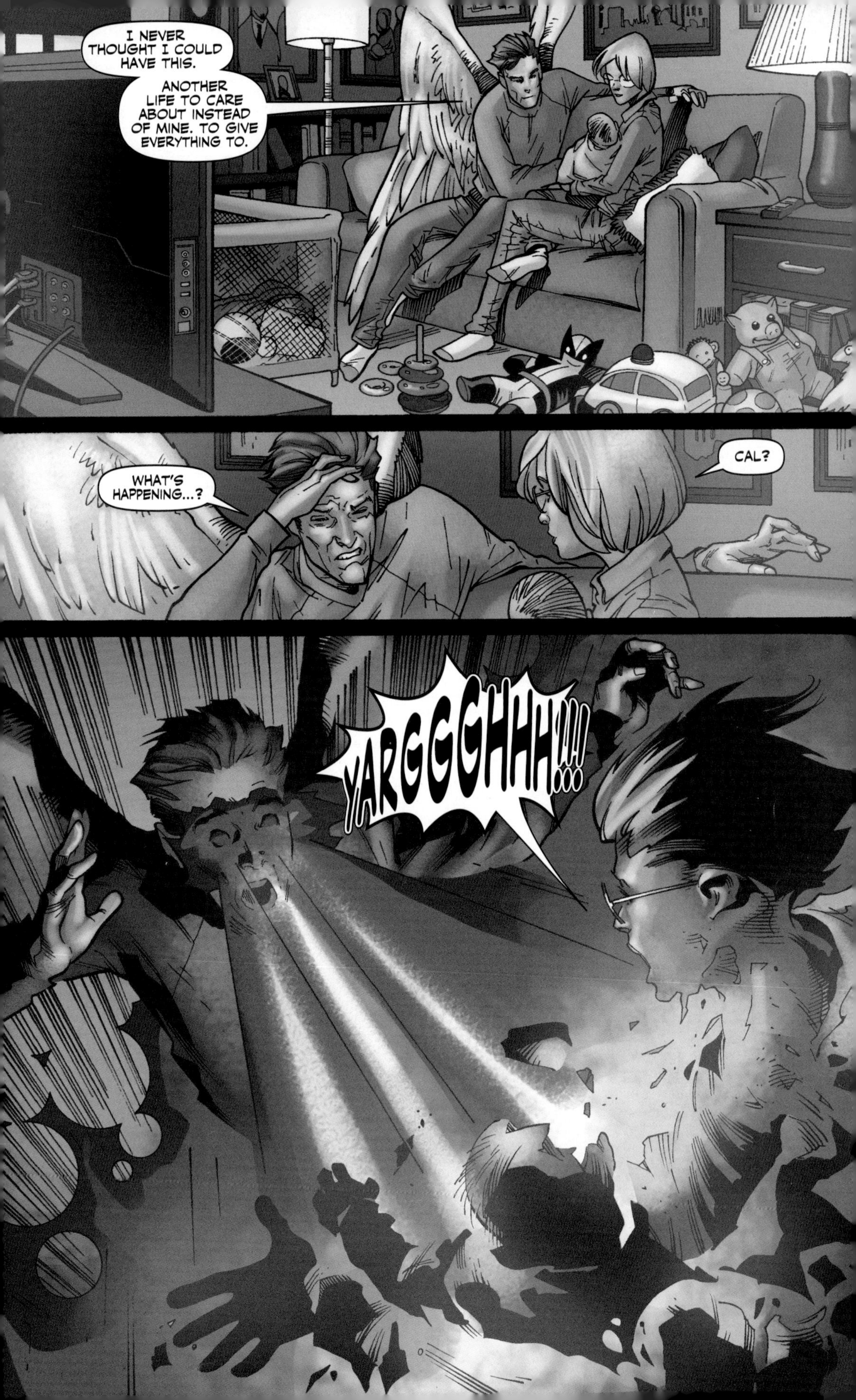
I NEVER THOUGHT I COULD HAVE THIS.
ANOTHER LIFE TO CARE ABOUT INSTEAD OF MINE. TO GIVE EVERYTHING TO.
WHAT'S HAPPENING...?
CAL?
YARGGGHHH!!!

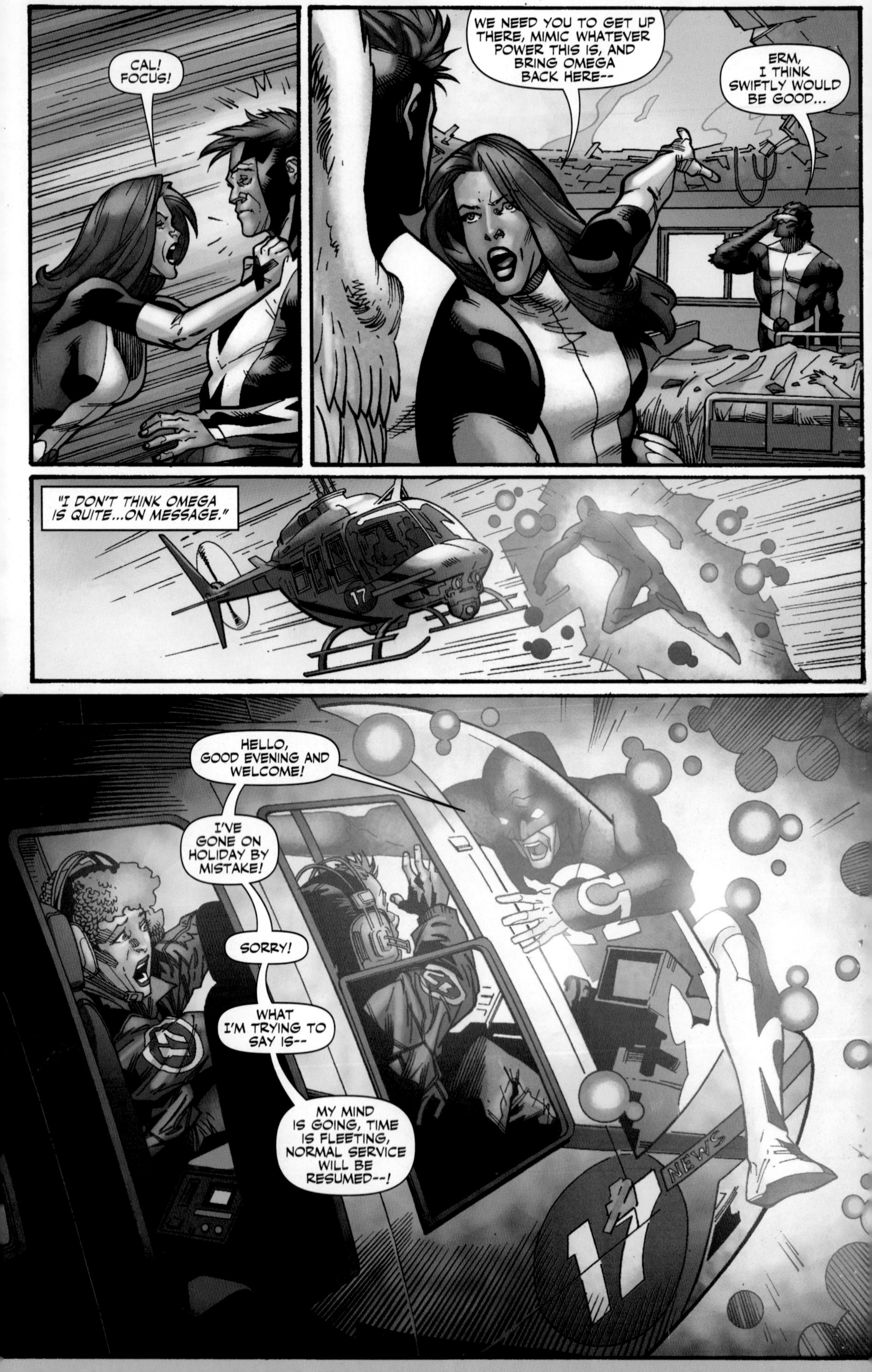
CAL! FOCUS!
WE NEED YOU TO GET UP THERE, MIMIC WHATEVER POWER THIS IS, AND BRING OMEGA BACK HERE--
ERM, I THINK SWIFTLY WOULD BE GOOD...
"I DON'T THINK OMEGA IS QUITE...ON MESSAGE."
HELLO, GOOD EVENING AND WELCOME!
I'VE GONE ON HOLIDAY BY MISTAKE!
SORRY!
WHAT I'M TRYING TO SAY IS--
MY MIND IS GOING, TIME IS FLEETING, NORMAL SERVICE WILL BE RESUMED--!
NEWS
17

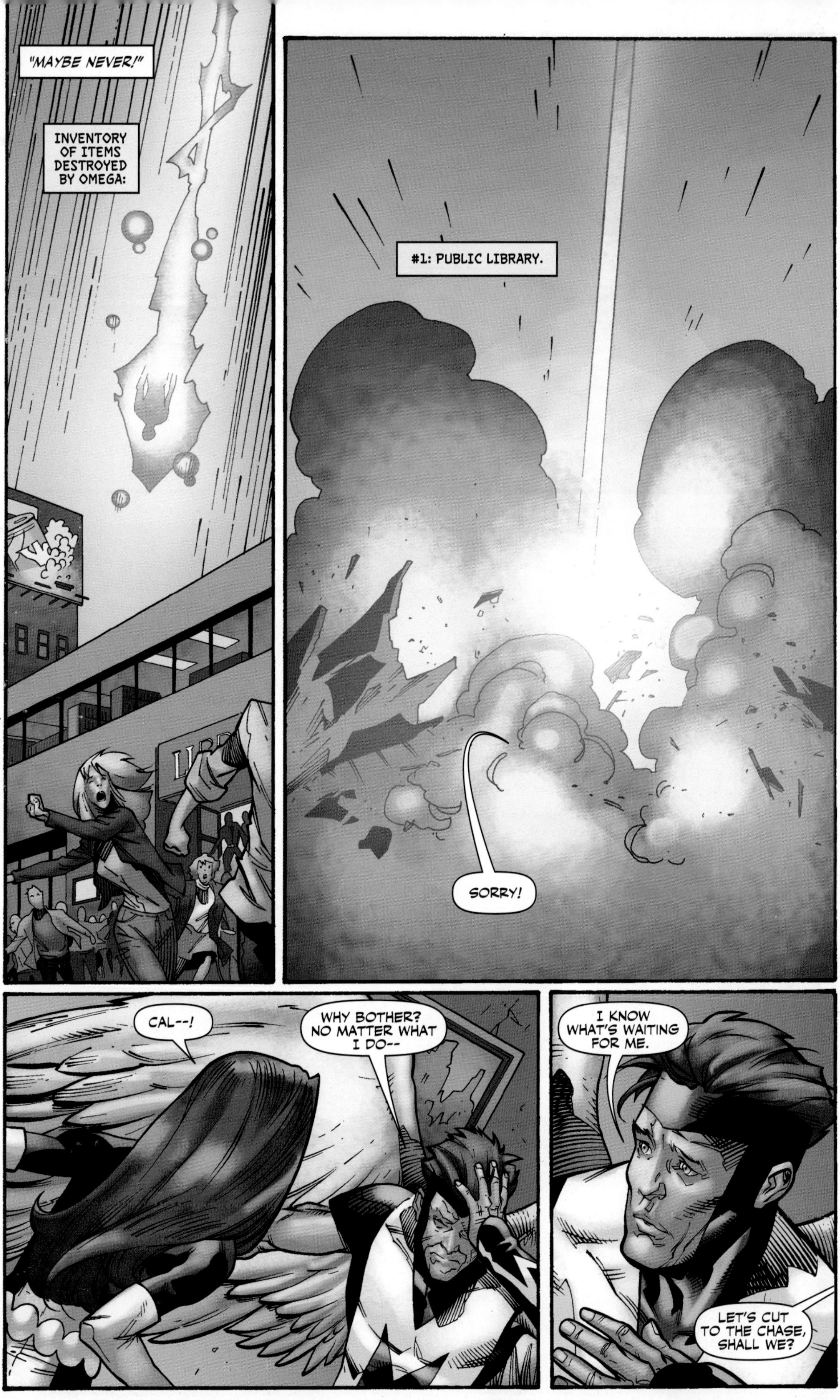
"MAYBE NEVER!"
INVENTORY OF ITEMS DESTROYED BY OMEGA:
#1: PUBLIC LIBRARY.
SORRY!
CAL--!
WHY BOTHER? NO MATTER WHAT I DO--
I KNOW WHAT'S WAITING FOR ME.
LET'S CUT TO THE CHASE, SHALL WE?

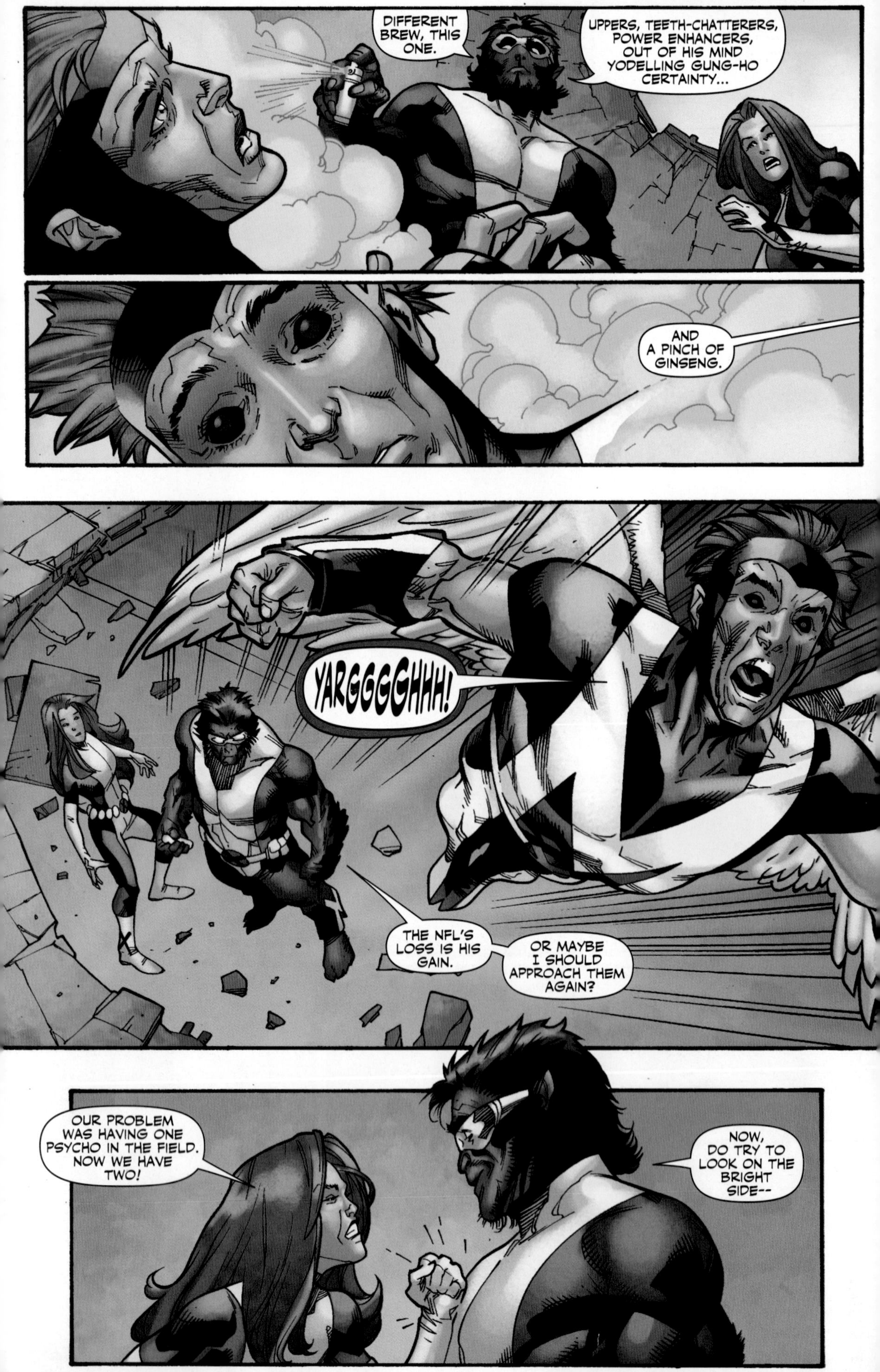
DIFFERENT BREW, THIS ONE.
UPPERS, TEETH-CHATTERERS, POWER ENHANCERS, OUT OF HIS MIND YODELLING GUNG-HO CERTAINTY...
AND A PINCH OF GINSENG.
YARGGGGHHH!
THE NFL'S LOSS IS HIS GAIN.
OR MAYBE I SHOULD APPROACH THEM AGAIN?
OUR PROBLEM WAS HAVING ONE PSYCHO IN THE FIELD. NOW WE HAVE TWO!
NOW, DO TRY TO LOOK ON THE BRIGHT SIDE--

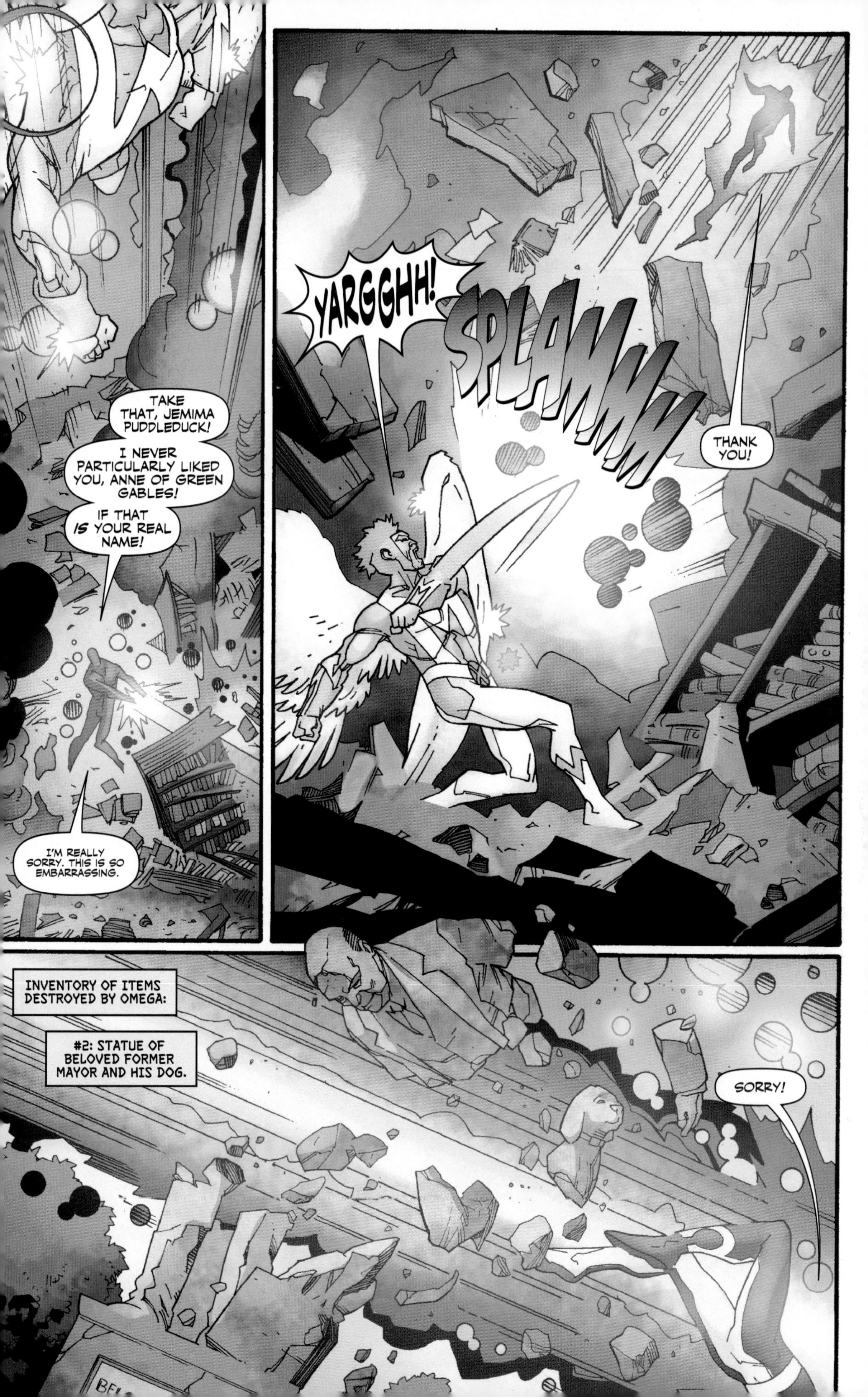
TAKE THAT, JEMIMA PUDDLEDUCK!
I NEVER PARTICULARLY LIKED YOU, ANNE OF GREEN GABLES!
IF THAT *IS* YOUR REAL NAME!
I'M REALLY SORRY. THIS IS SO EMBARRASSING.
YARGGHH!
SPLAMMM
THANK YOU!
INVENTORY OF ITEMS DESTROYED BY OMEGA:
#2: STATUE OF BELOVED FORMER MAYOR AND HIS DOG.
SORRY!

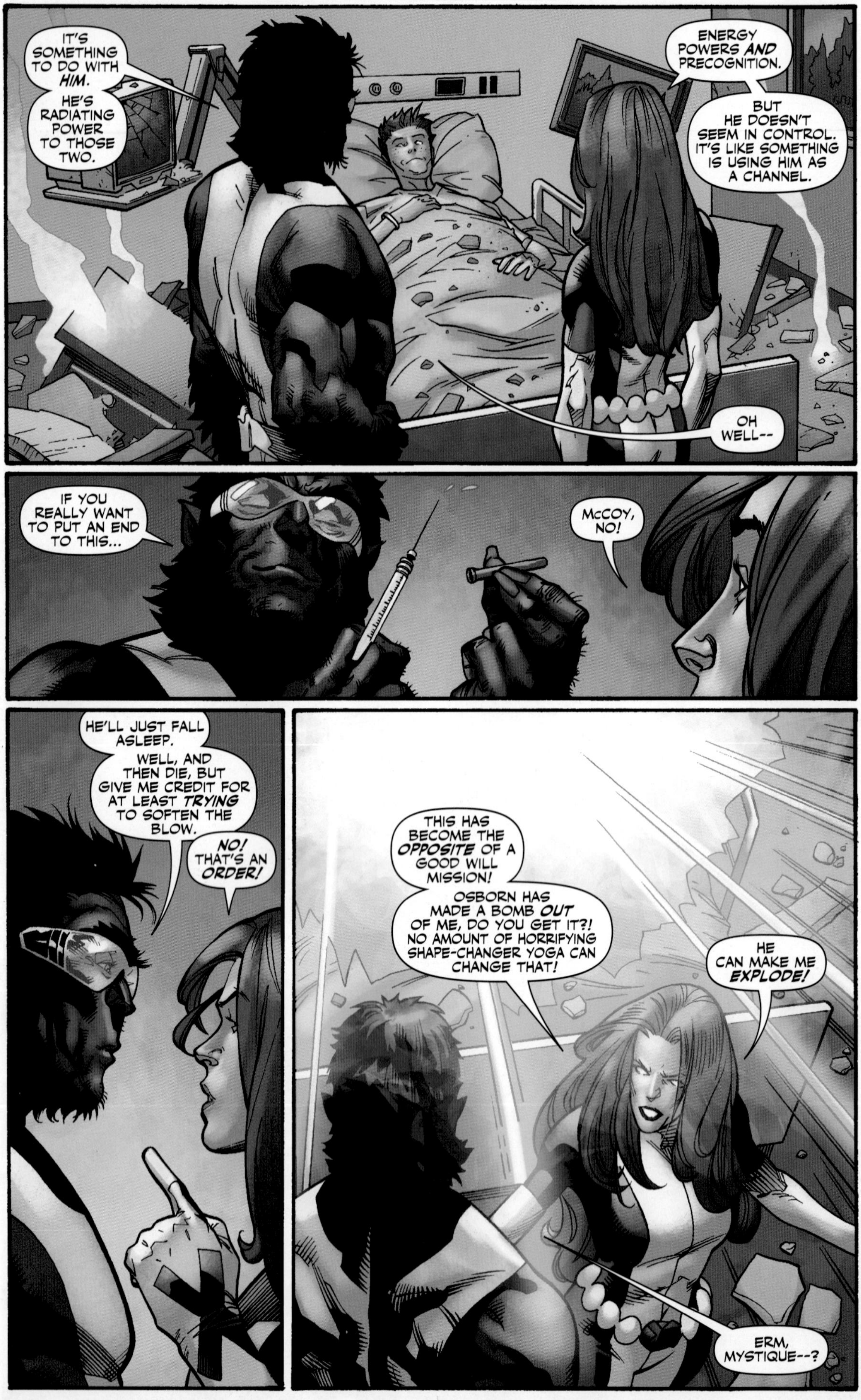
IT'S SOMETHING TO DO WITH *HIM*.
HE'S RADIATING POWER TO THOSE TWO.
ENERGY POWERS *AND* PRECOGNITION.
BUT HE DOESN'T SEEM IN CONTROL. IT'S LIKE SOMETHING IS USING HIM AS A CHANNEL.
OH WELL--
IF YOU REALLY WANT TO PUT AN END TO THIS...
McCOY, NO!
HE'LL JUST FALL ASLEEP.
WELL, AND THEN DIE, BUT GIVE ME CREDIT FOR AT LEAST *TRYING* TO SOFTEN THE BLOW.
NO! THAT'S AN *ORDER!*
THIS HAS BECOME THE *OPPOSITE* OF A GOOD WILL MISSION!
OSBORN HAS MADE A BOMB *OUT* OF ME, DO YOU GET IT?! NO AMOUNT OF HORRIFYING SHAPE-CHANGER YOGA CAN CHANGE THAT!
HE CAN MAKE ME *EXPLODE!*
ERM, MYSTIQUE--?

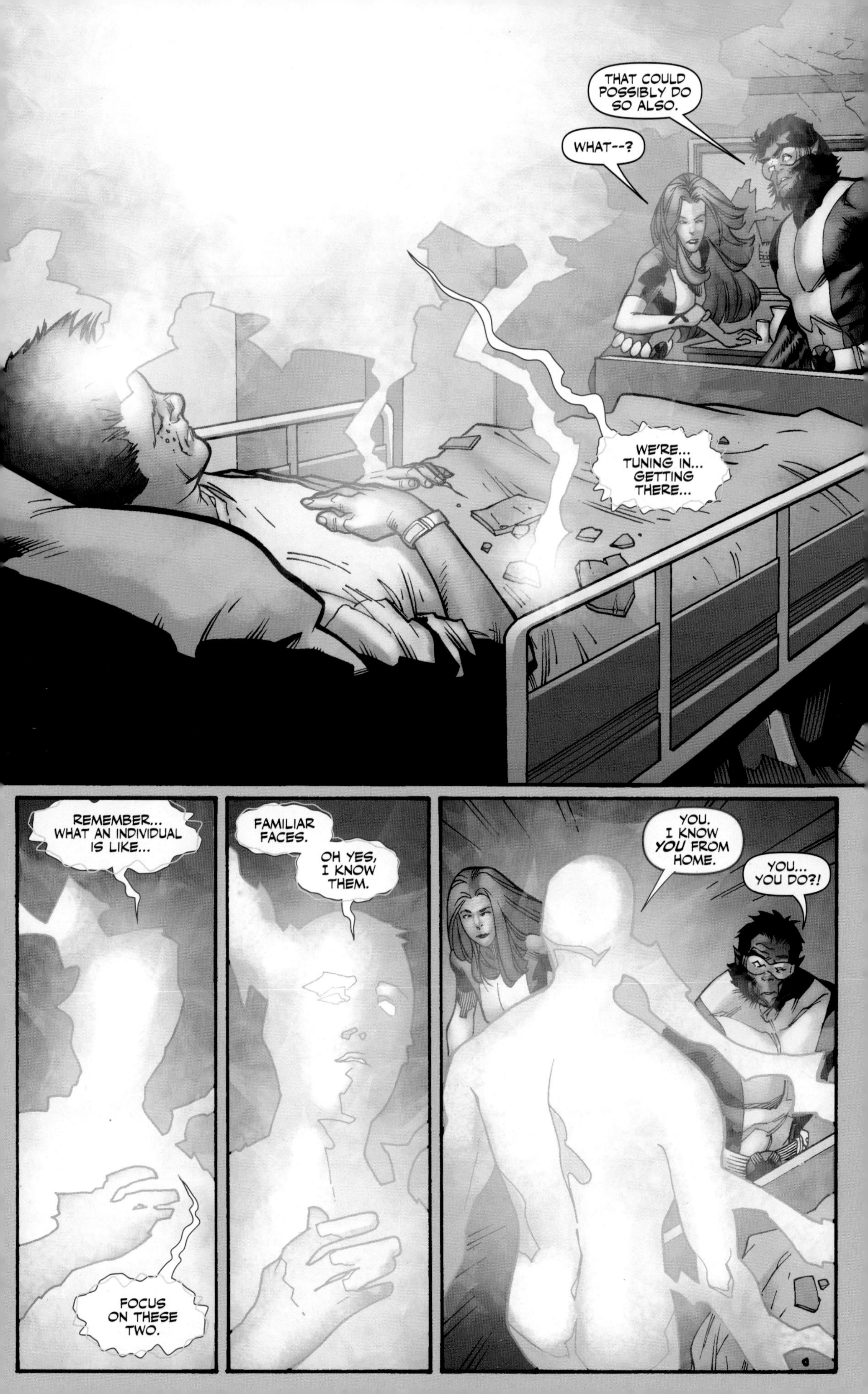
THAT COULD POSSIBLY DO SO ALSO.
WHAT--?
WE'RE... TUNING IN... GETTING THERE...
REMEMBER... WHAT AN INDIVIDUAL IS LIKE...
FOCUS ON THESE TWO.
FAMILIAR FACES.
OH YES, I KNOW THEM.
YOU. I KNOW YOU FROM HOME.
YOU... YOU DO?!

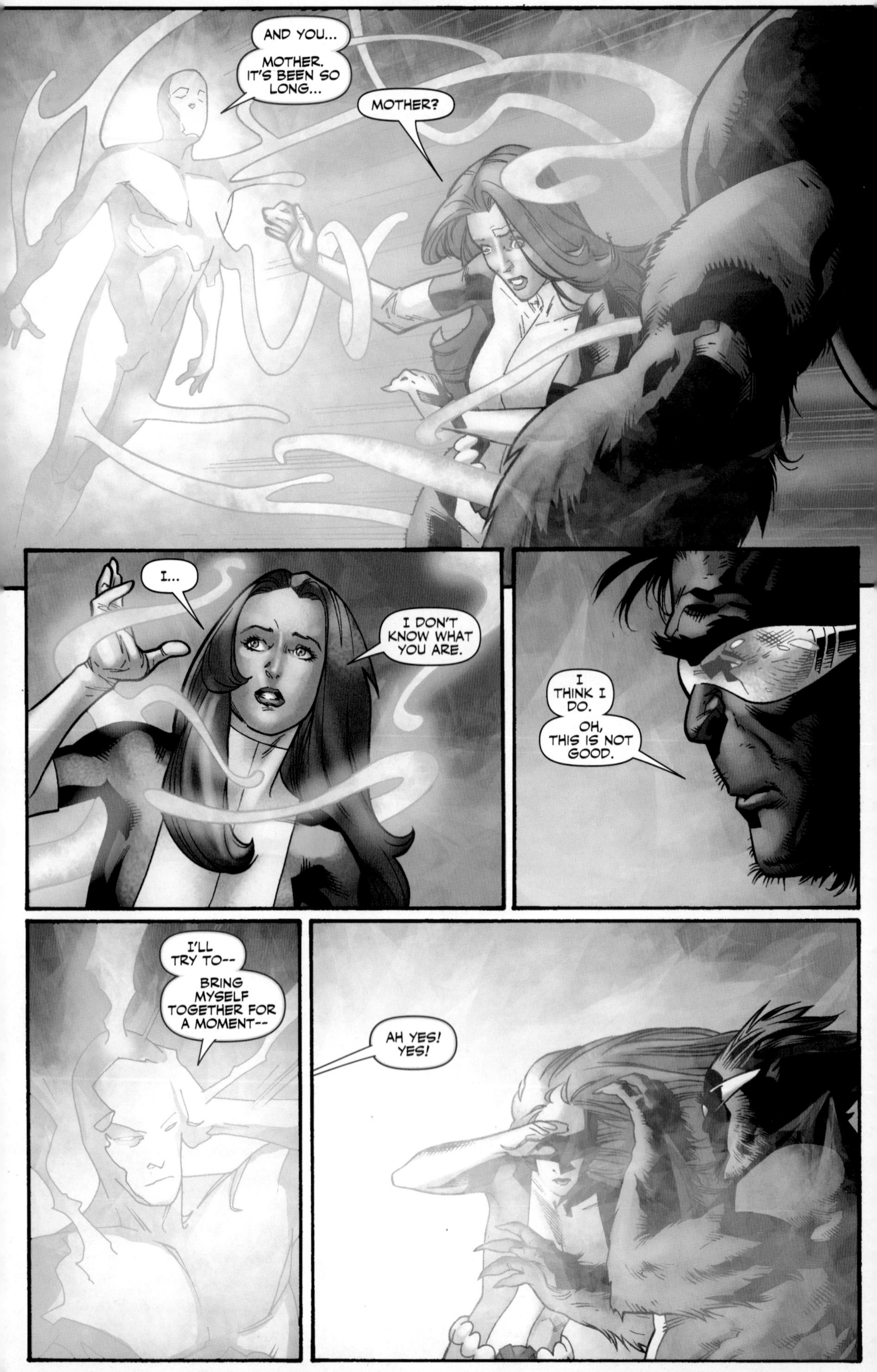
AND YOU...
MOTHER. IT'S BEEN SO LONG...
MOTHER?
I...
I DON'T KNOW WHAT YOU ARE.
I THINK I DO.
OH, THIS IS NOT GOOD.
I'LL TRY TO--
BRING MYSELF TOGETHER FOR A MOMENT--
AH YES! YES!

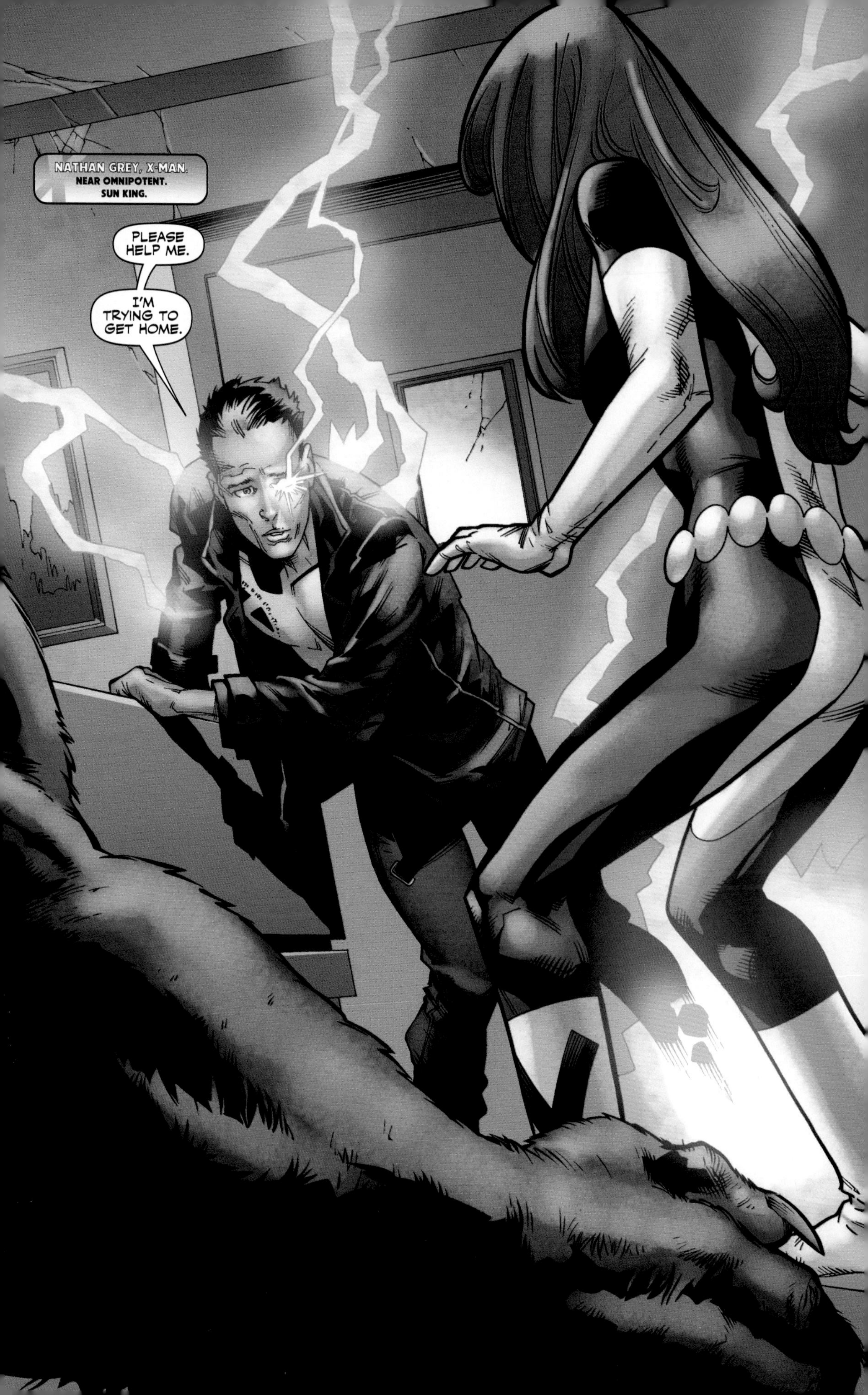
NATHAN GREY, X-MAN.
NEAR OMNIPOTENT.
SUN KING.
PLEASE HELP ME.
I'M TRYING TO GET HOME.

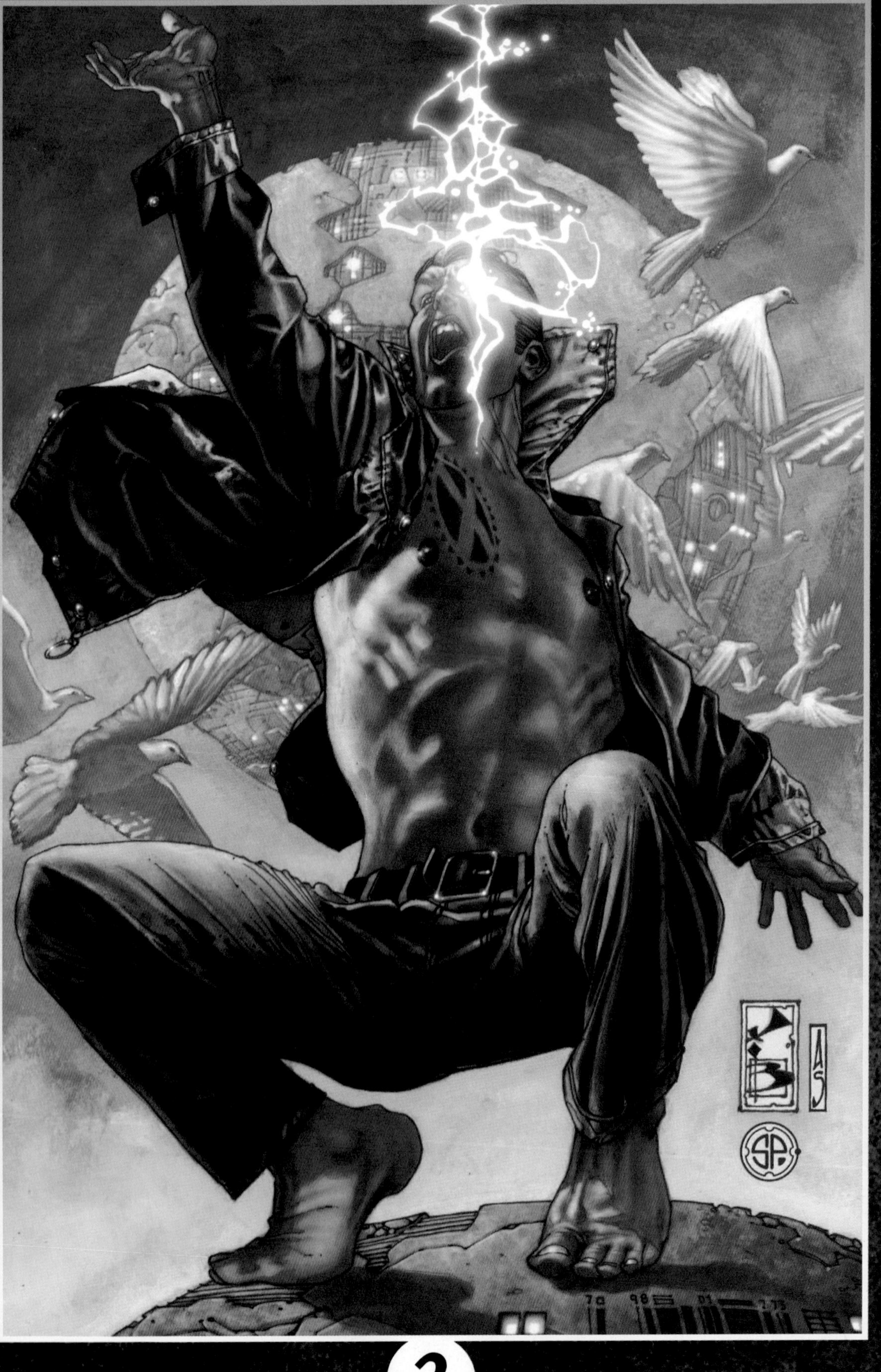

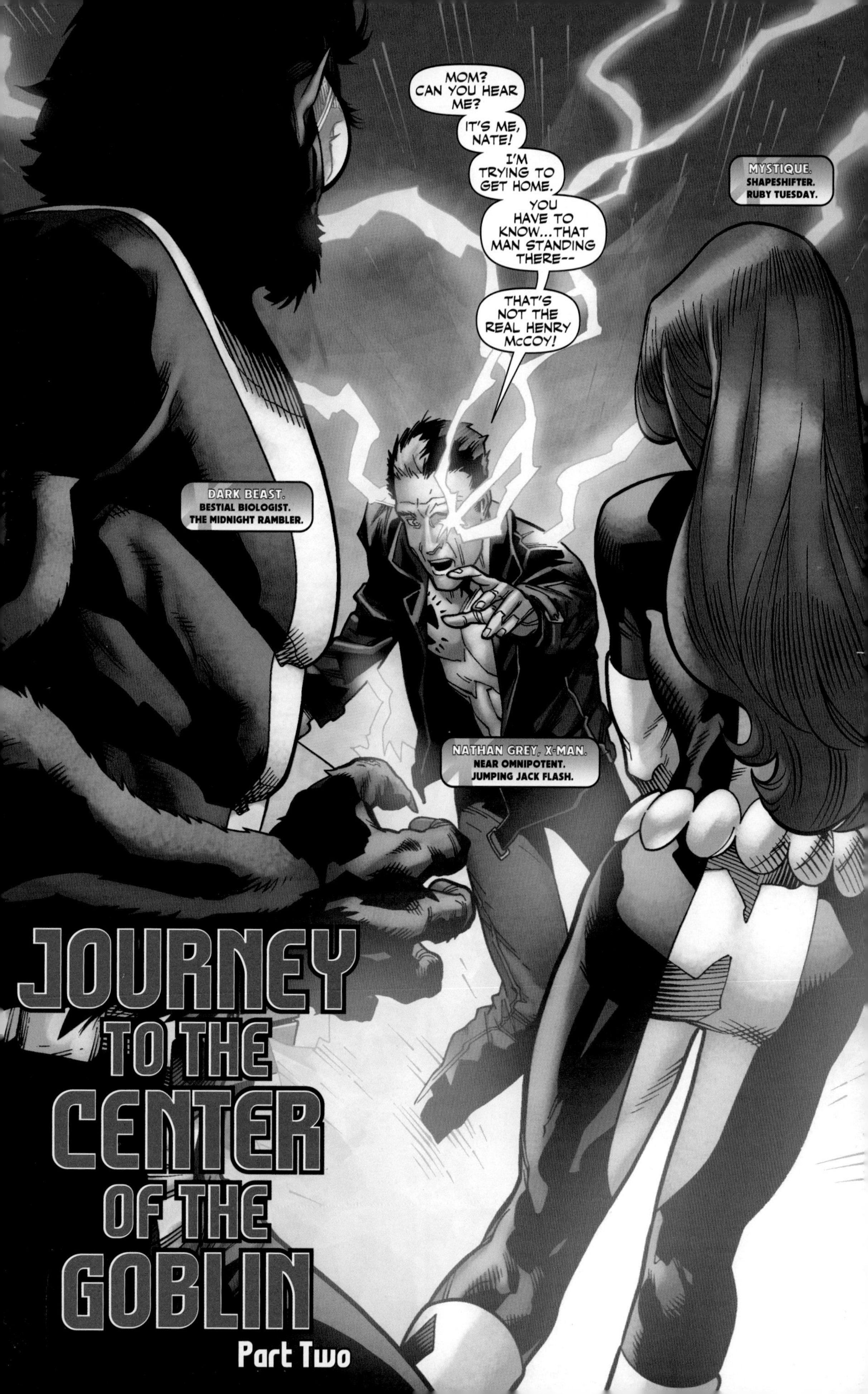
MOM? CAN YOU HEAR ME?
IT'S ME, NATE!
I'M TRYING TO GET HOME.
YOU HAVE TO KNOW...THAT MAN STANDING THERE--
THAT'S NOT THE REAL HENRY McCOY!
MYSTIQUE. SHAPESHIFTER. RUBY TUESDAY.
DARK BEAST. BESTIAL BIOLOGIST. THE MIDNIGHT RAMBLER.
NATHAN GREY, X-MAN. NEAR OMNIPOTENT. JUMPING JACK FLASH.
JOURNEY TO THE CENTER OF THE GOBLIN
Part Two

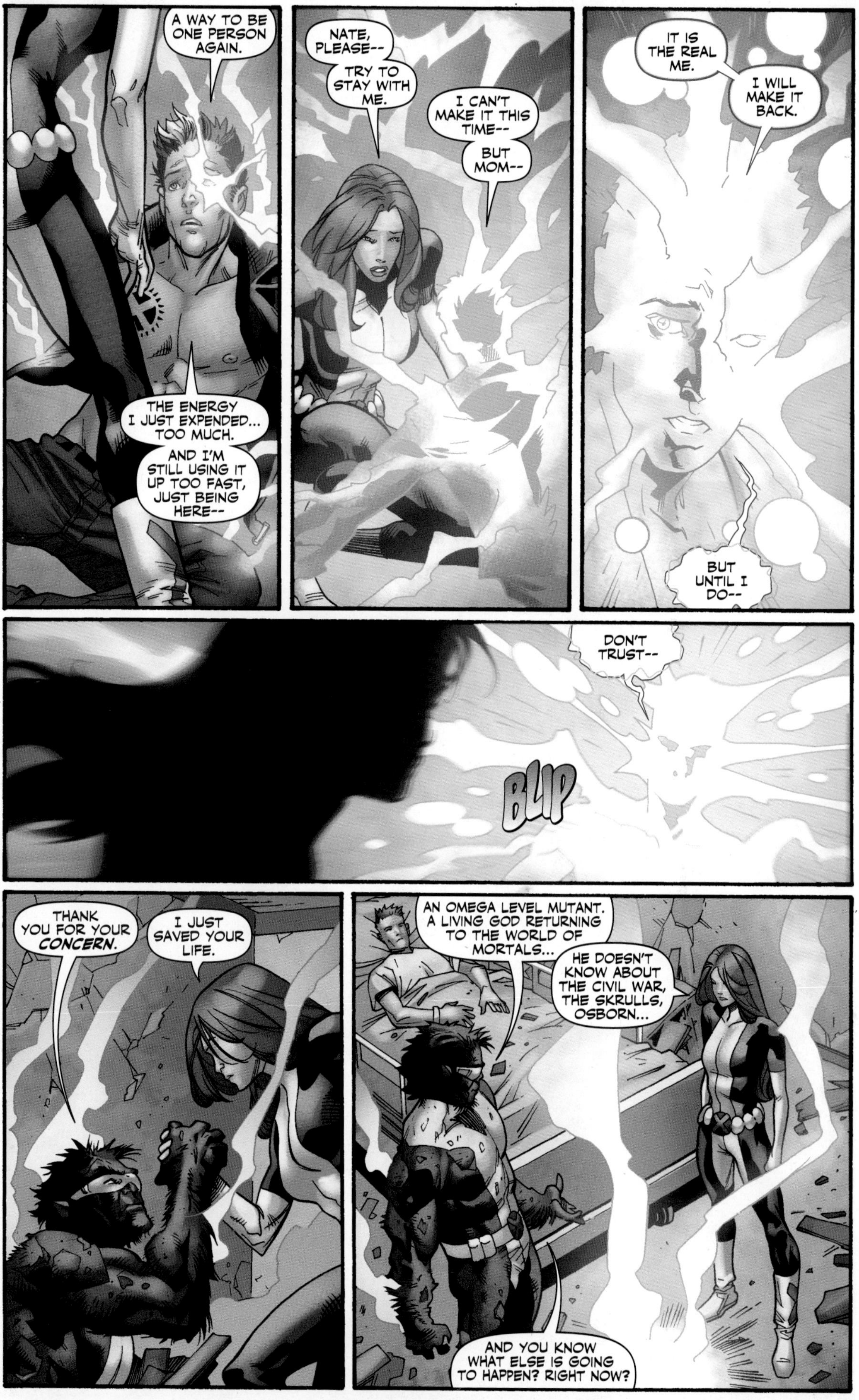
A WAY TO BE ONE PERSON AGAIN.
THE ENERGY I JUST EXPENDED... TOO MUCH.
AND I'M STILL USING IT UP TOO FAST, JUST BEING HERE--
NATE, PLEASE--
TRY TO STAY WITH ME.
I CAN'T MAKE IT THIS TIME--
BUT MOM--
IT IS THE REAL ME.
I WILL MAKE IT BACK.
BUT UNTIL I DO--
DON'T TRUST--
BLIP
THANK YOU FOR YOUR *CONCERN*.
I JUST SAVED YOUR LIFE.
AN OMEGA LEVEL MUTANT. A LIVING GOD RETURNING TO THE WORLD OF MORTALS...
HE DOESN'T KNOW ABOUT THE CIVIL WAR, THE SKRULLS, OSBORN...
AND YOU KNOW WHAT ELSE IS GOING TO HAPPEN? RIGHT NOW?

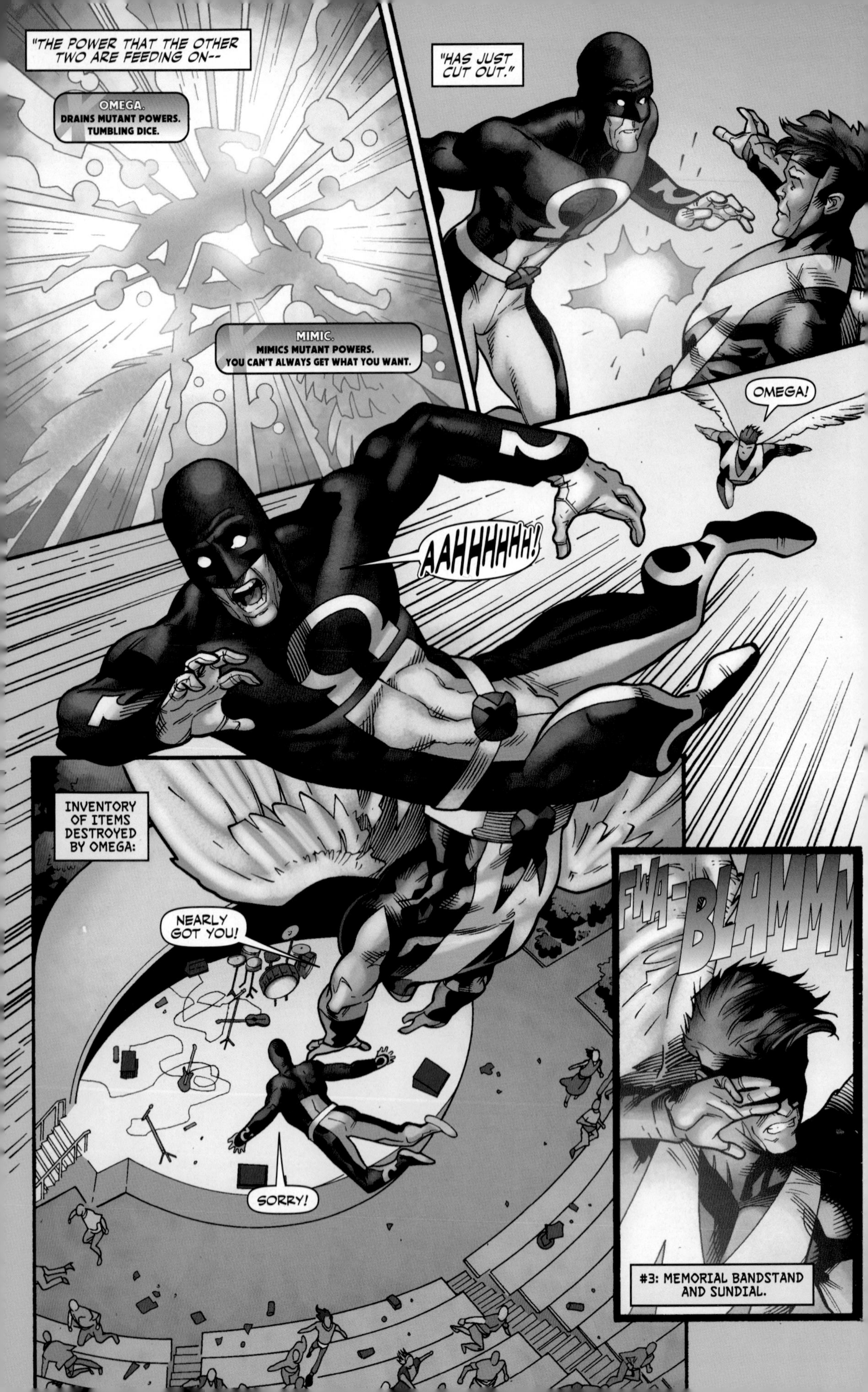
"THE POWER THAT THE OTHER TWO ARE FEEDING ON--
OMEGA. DRAINS MUTANT POWERS. TUMBLING DICE.
MIMIC. MIMICS MUTANT POWERS. YOU CAN'T ALWAYS GET WHAT YOU WANT.
"HAS JUST CUT OUT."
OMEGA!
AAHHHHHH!
INVENTORY OF ITEMS DESTROYED BY OMEGA:
NEARLY GOT YOU!
SORRY!
FWA-BLAMMM
#3: MEMORIAL BANDSTAND AND SUNDIAL.

WELL...

NORMAN OSBORN.
OUR TITLE STAR, WE'LL GET TO THAT.
A MAN OF WEALTH AND TASTE.

THAT WORKED OUT ON THE CREDIT SIDE.

THE TOWN BELIEVED OUR STORY ABOUT AN ALIEN FORCE POSSESSING PEOPLE. IT TOOK OVER OMEGA. HE BEAT IT.

THEY'RE GOING TO BUILD *STATUES* OF YOU.

XAVIER, SUMMERS, THEY *LIVED* FOR THIS MOMENT. BUT I GOT IT.

BUT! TO BUSINESS! WHO *IS* THIS X-MAN?

HE'S FROM THE SAME ALTERNATE REALITY AS DR. McCOY.

HE STYLES HIMSELF AS A "MUTANT SHAMAN," IDENTIFYING ENTIRELY WITH THAT CAUSE.

WHICH WOULD NORMALLY MAKE ME KEEN TO BRING HIM ONBOARD. HOWEVER--

PRECOGNITION. TELEPATHY. TELEKINESIS. ENERGY MANIPULATION POWERS ON A VAST SCALE...

A CERTAIN UNPREDICTABILITY... A CERTAIN WILDNESS OF THOUGHT... AND A *SUMMERS*, TOO.

HE COULD GO ONE-ON-ONE WITH THE *SENTRY*--

WHICH HAS ALWAYS BEEN HOW I JUDGE--

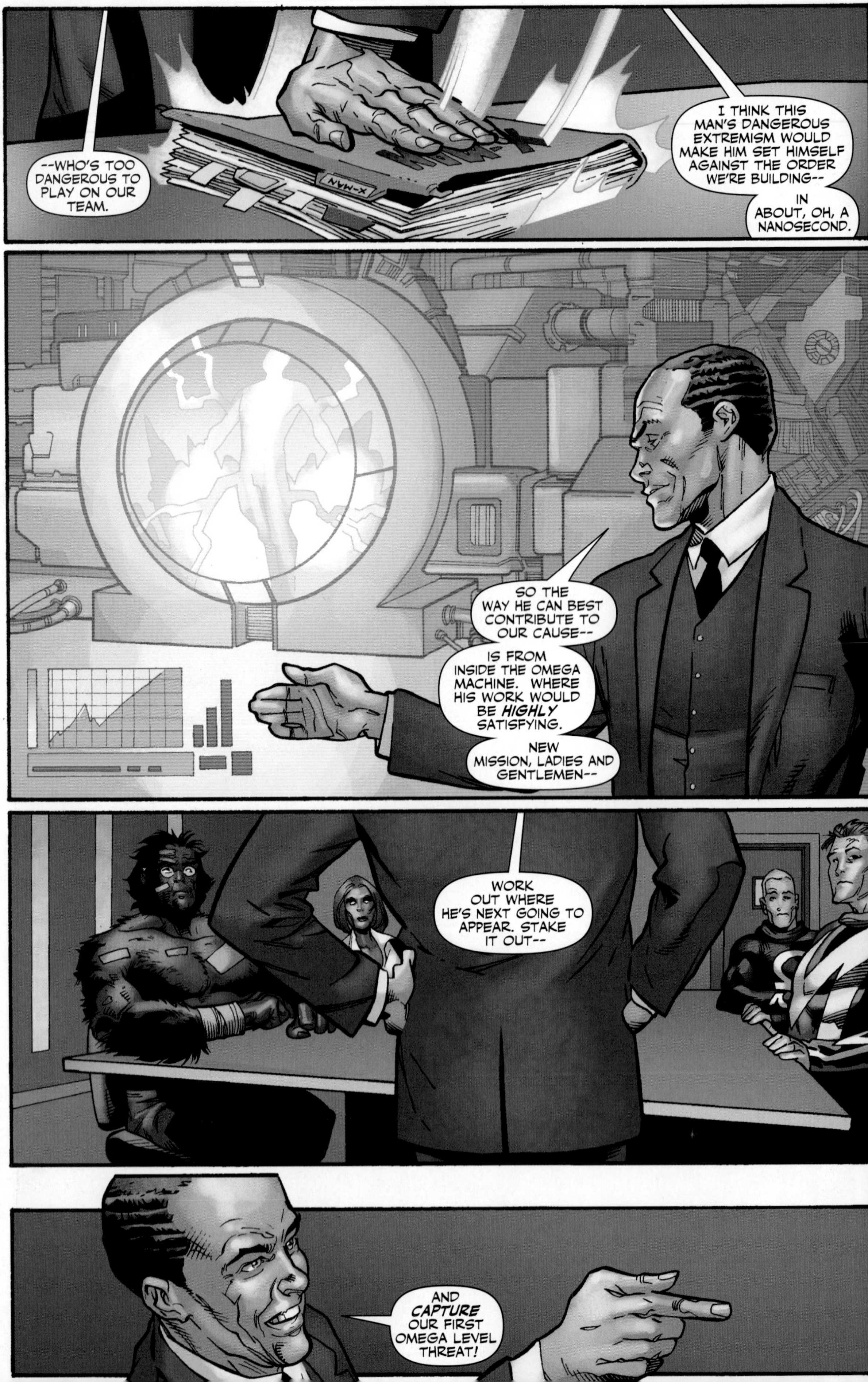
--WHO'S TOO DANGEROUS TO PLAY ON OUR TEAM.
X-MAN
I THINK THIS MAN'S DANGEROUS EXTREMISM WOULD MAKE HIM SET HIMSELF AGAINST THE ORDER WE'RE BUILDING--
IN ABOUT, OH, A NANOSECOND.
SO THE WAY HE CAN BEST CONTRIBUTE TO OUR CAUSE--
IS FROM INSIDE THE OMEGA MACHINE. WHERE HIS WORK WOULD BE *HIGHLY* SATISFYING.
NEW MISSION, LADIES AND GENTLEMEN--
WORK OUT WHERE HE'S NEXT GOING TO APPEAR. STAKE IT OUT--
AND *CAPTURE* OUR FIRST OMEGA LEVEL THREAT!

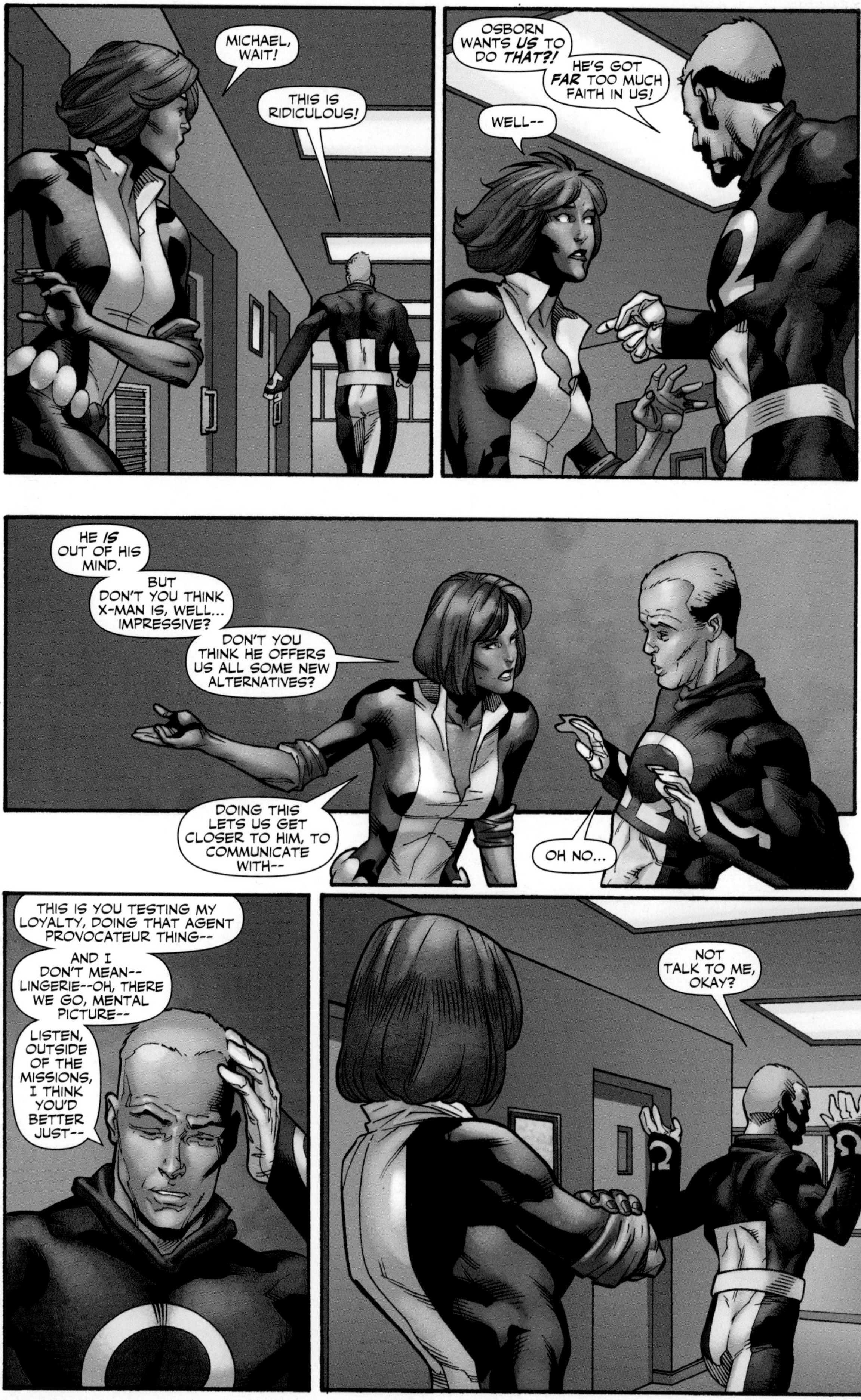
MICHAEL, WAIT!
THIS IS RIDICULOUS!
OSBORN WANTS US TO DO THAT?!
HE'S GOT FAR TOO MUCH FAITH IN US!
WELL--
HE IS OUT OF HIS MIND.
BUT DON'T YOU THINK X-MAN IS, WELL... IMPRESSIVE?
DON'T YOU THINK HE OFFERS US ALL SOME NEW ALTERNATIVES?
DOING THIS LETS US GET CLOSER TO HIM, TO COMMUNICATE WITH--
OH NO...
THIS IS YOU TESTING MY LOYALTY, DOING THAT AGENT PROVOCATEUR THING--
AND I DON'T MEAN--LINGERIE--OH, THERE WE GO, MENTAL PICTURE--
LISTEN, OUTSIDE OF THE MISSIONS, I THINK YOU'D BETTER JUST--
NOT TALK TO ME, OKAY?

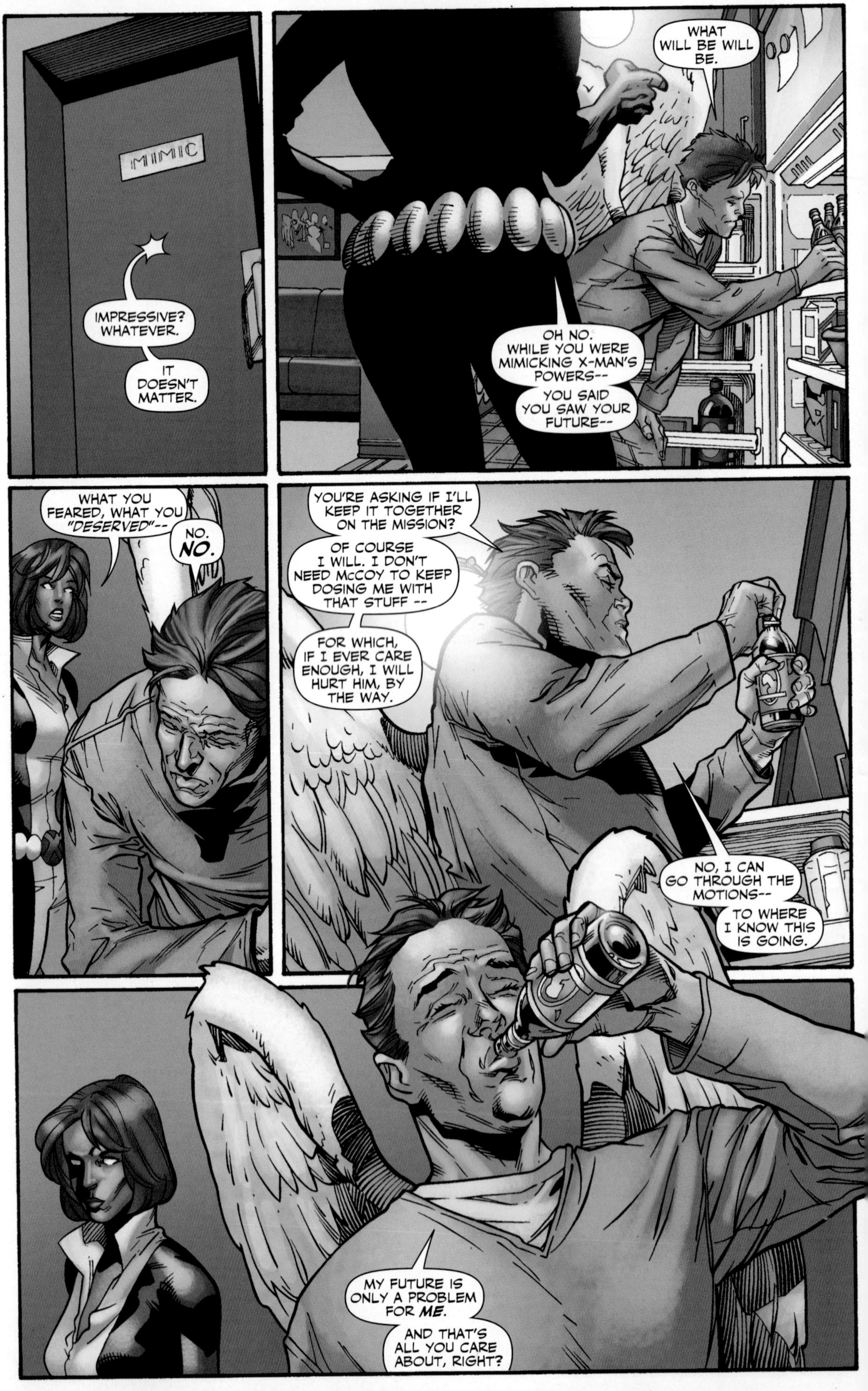
MIMIC
IMPRESSIVE? WHATEVER.
IT DOESN'T MATTER.
WHAT WILL BE WILL BE.
OH NO. WHILE YOU WERE MIMICKING X-MAN'S POWERS--
YOU SAID YOU SAW YOUR FUTURE--
WHAT YOU FEARED, WHAT YOU "DESERVED"--
NO. NO.
YOU'RE ASKING IF I'LL KEEP IT TOGETHER ON THE MISSION?
OF COURSE I WILL. I DON'T NEED McCOY TO KEEP DOSING ME WITH THAT STUFF --
FOR WHICH, IF I EVER CARE ENOUGH, I WILL HURT HIM, BY THE WAY.
NO, I CAN GO THROUGH THE MOTIONS--
TO WHERE I KNOW THIS IS GOING.
MY FUTURE IS ONLY A PROBLEM FOR ME.
AND THAT'S ALL YOU CARE ABOUT, RIGHT?

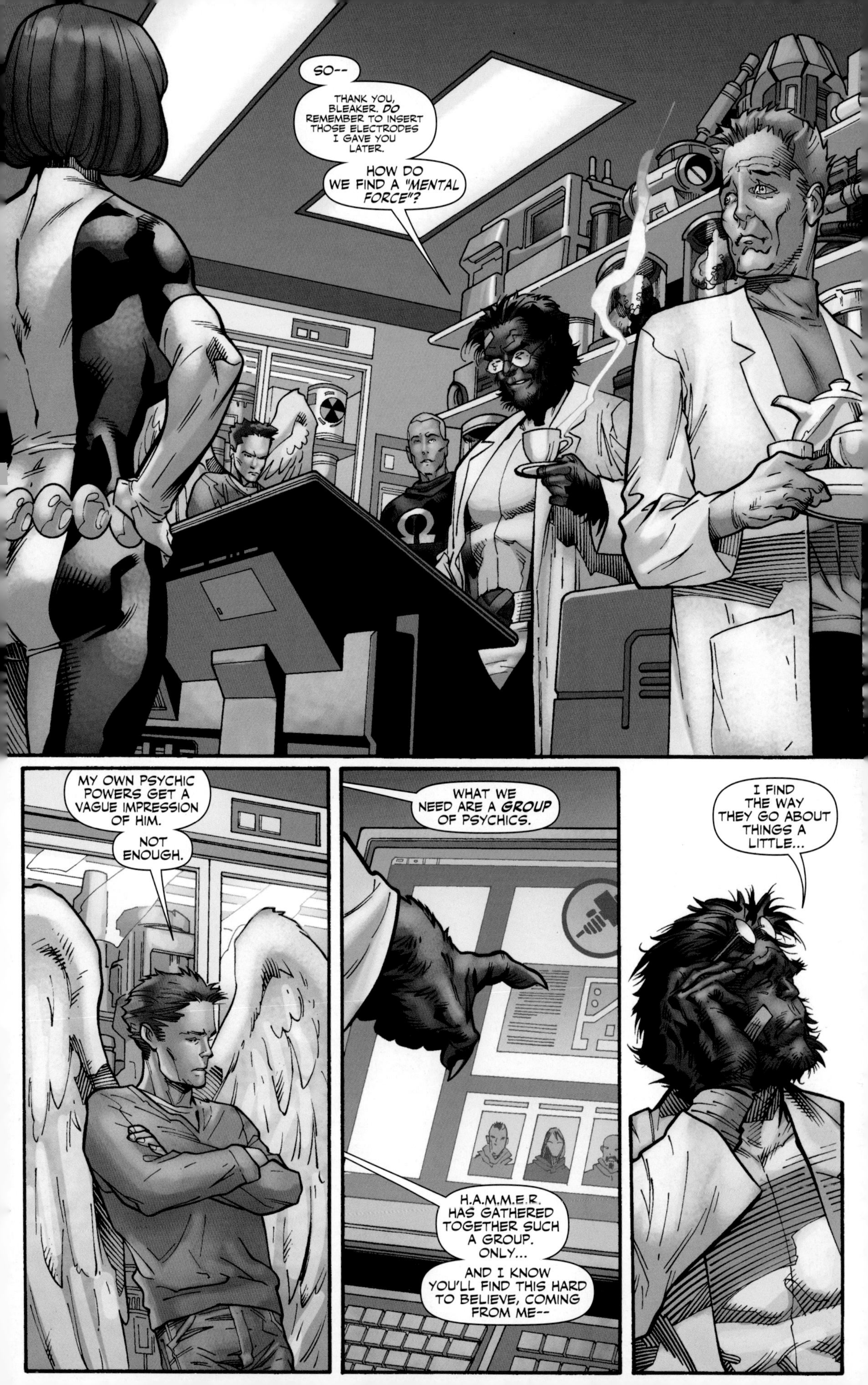
SO--
THANK YOU, BLEAKER. DO REMEMBER TO INSERT THOSE ELECTRODES I GAVE YOU LATER.
HOW DO WE FIND A "MENTAL FORCE"?
MY OWN PSYCHIC POWERS GET A VAGUE IMPRESSION OF HIM.
NOT ENOUGH.
WHAT WE NEED ARE A GROUP OF PSYCHICS.
H.A.M.M.E.R. HAS GATHERED TOGETHER SUCH A GROUP. ONLY...
AND I KNOW YOU'LL FIND THIS HARD TO BELIEVE, COMING FROM ME--
I FIND THE WAY THEY GO ABOUT THINGS A LITTLE...

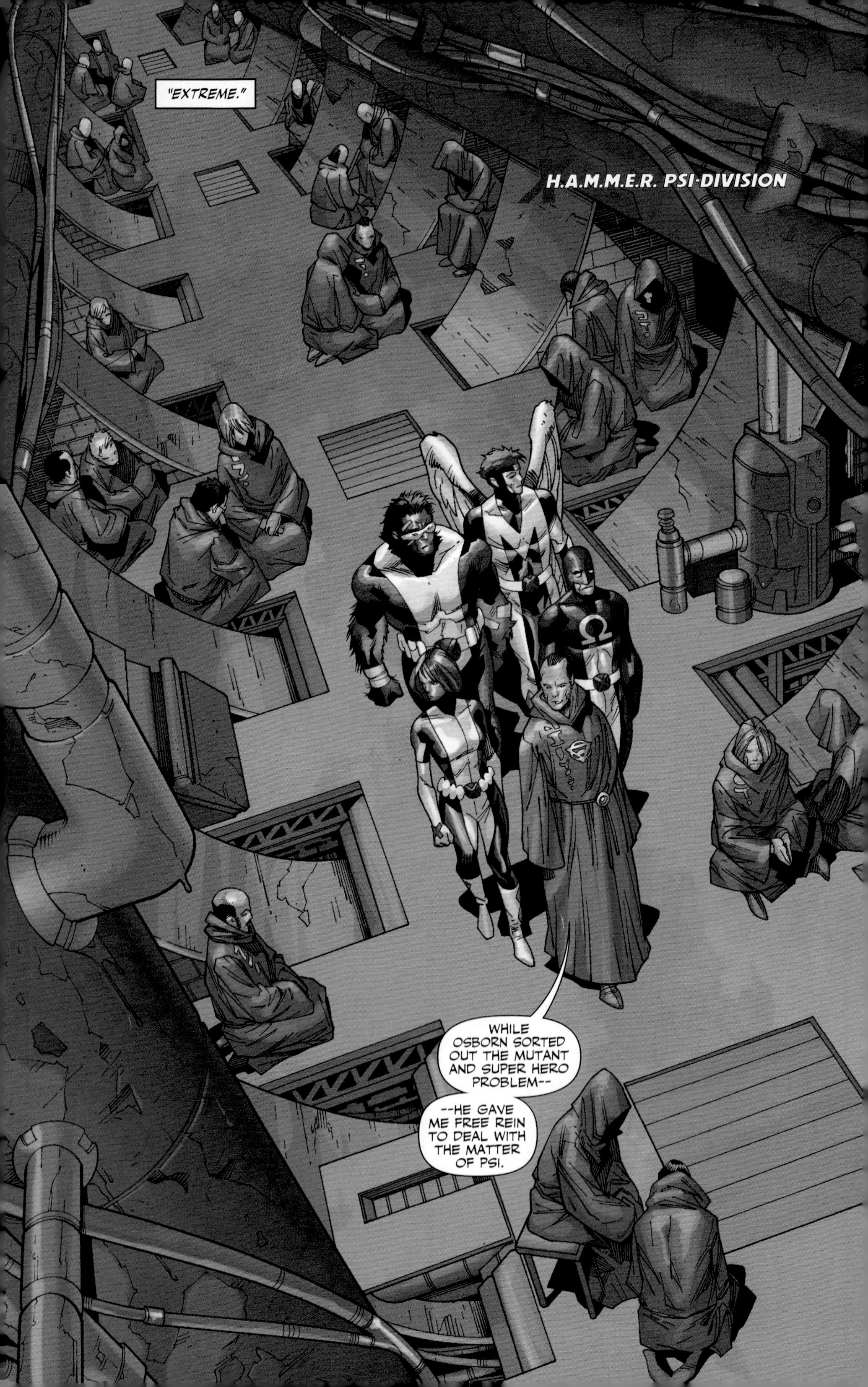
"EXTREME."
H.A.M.M.E.R. PSI-DIVISION
WHILE OSBORN SORTED OUT THE MUTANT AND SUPER HERO PROBLEM--
--HE GAVE ME FREE REIN TO DEAL WITH THE MATTER OF PSI.

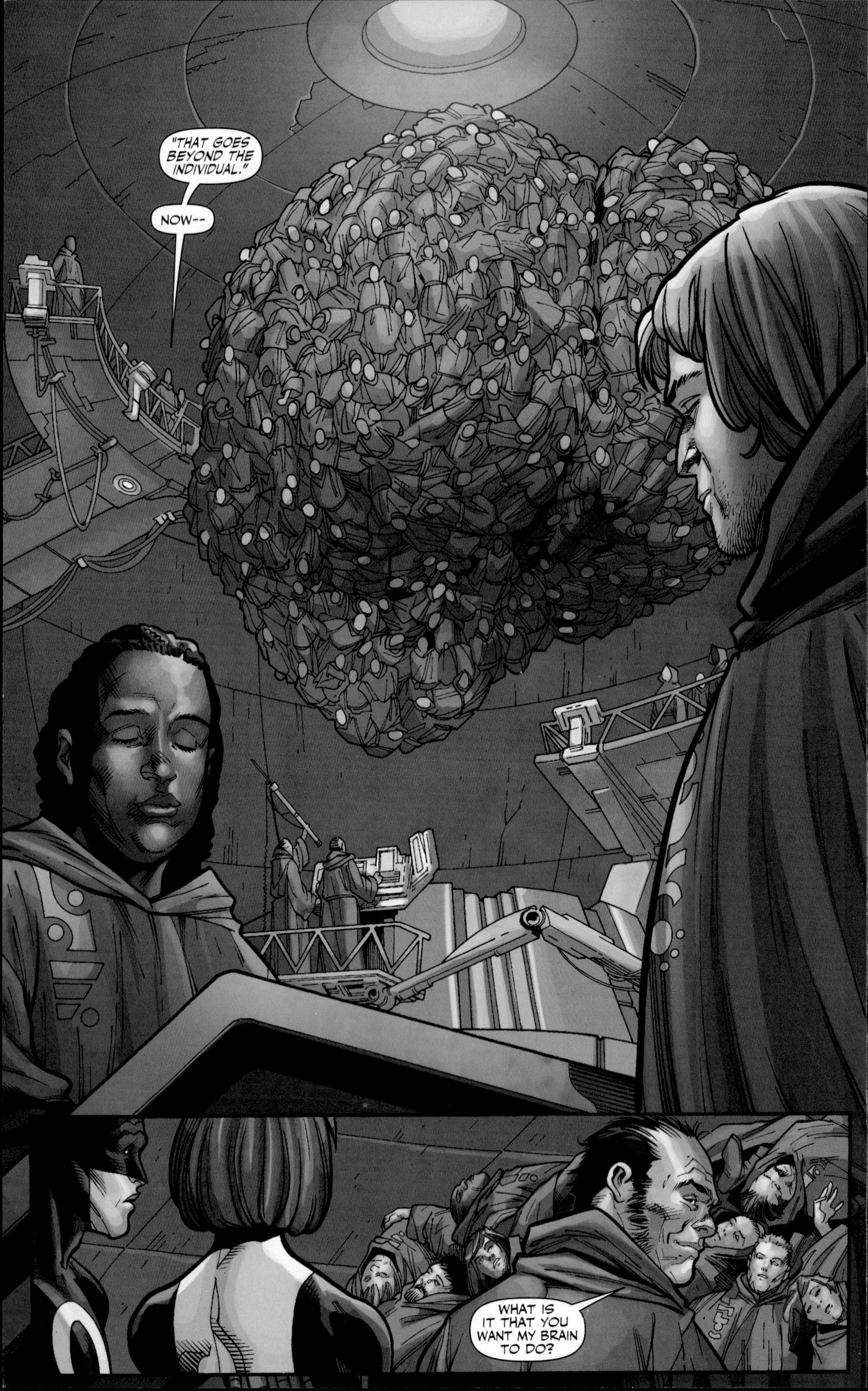
"THAT GOES BEYOND THE INDIVIDUAL."
NOW--
WHAT IS IT THAT YOU WANT MY BRAIN TO DO?

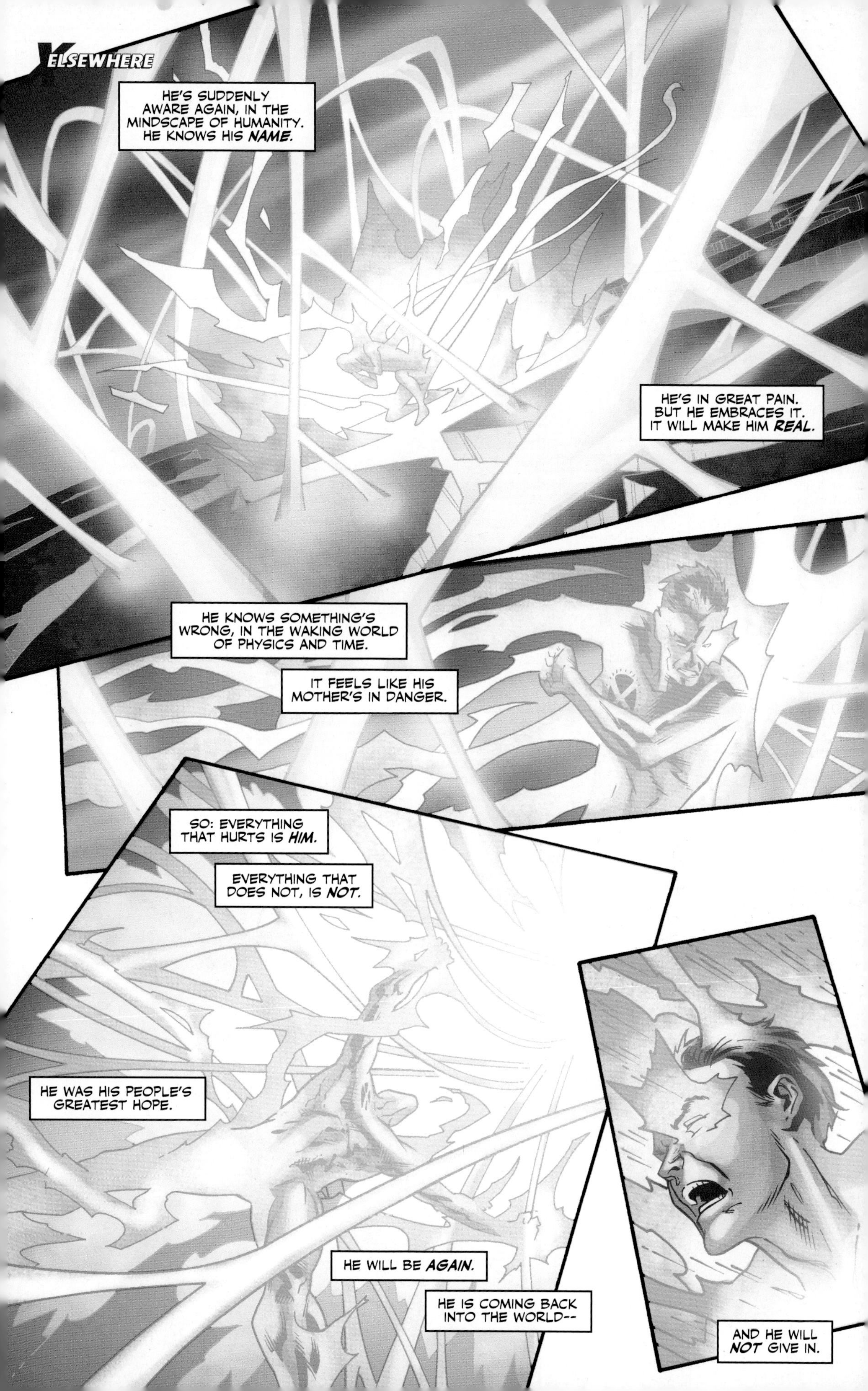
ELSEWHERE
HE'S SUDDENLY AWARE AGAIN, IN THE MINDSCAPE OF HUMANITY. HE KNOWS HIS NAME.
HE'S IN GREAT PAIN. BUT HE EMBRACES IT. IT WILL MAKE HIM REAL.
HE KNOWS SOMETHING'S WRONG, IN THE WAKING WORLD OF PHYSICS AND TIME.
IT FEELS LIKE HIS MOTHER'S IN DANGER.
SO: EVERYTHING THAT HURTS IS HIM.
EVERYTHING THAT DOES NOT, IS NOT.
HE WAS HIS PEOPLE'S GREATEST HOPE.
HE WILL BE AGAIN.
HE IS COMING BACK INTO THE WORLD--
AND HE WILL NOT GIVE IN.

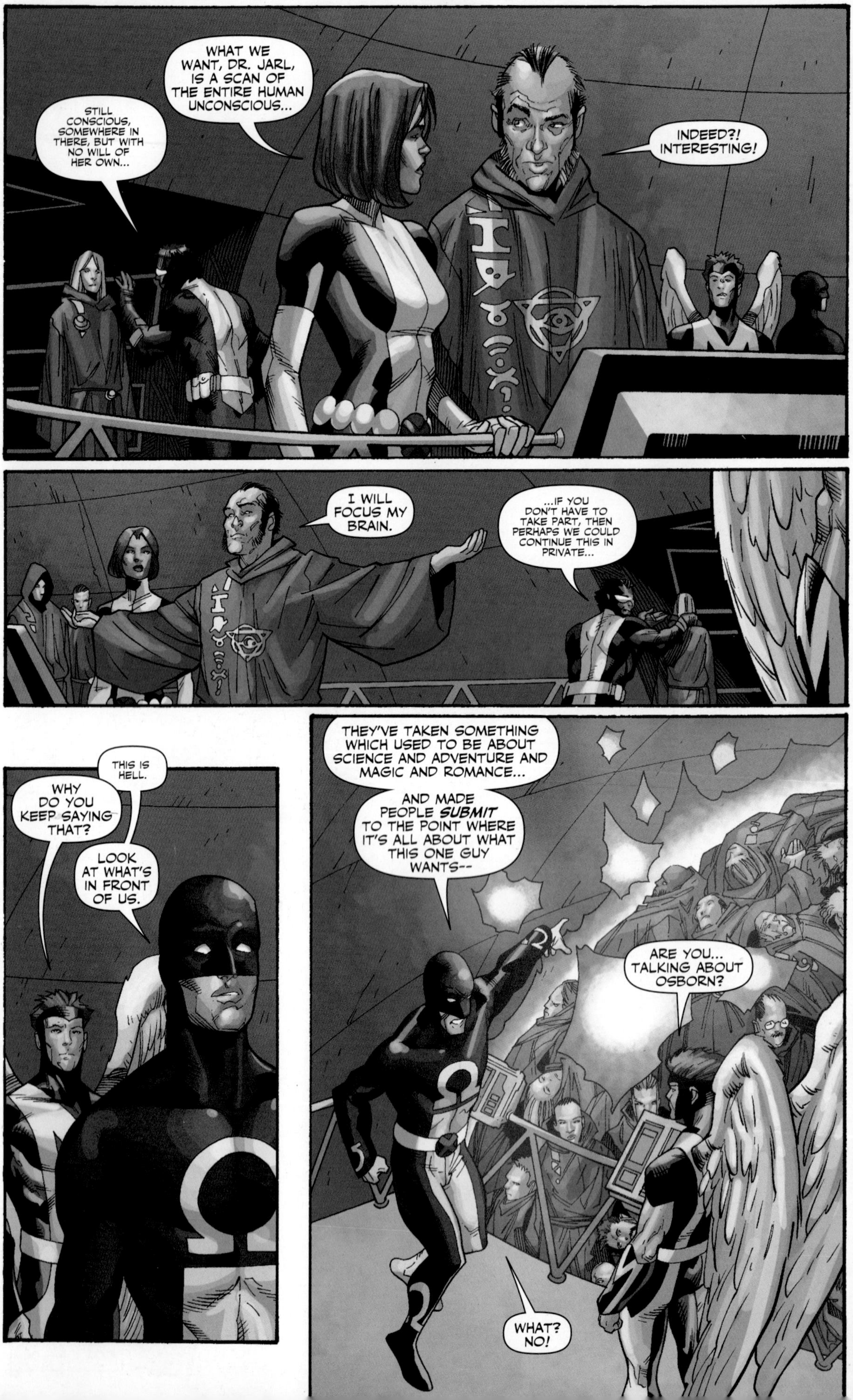
WHAT WE WANT, DR. JARL, IS A SCAN OF THE ENTIRE HUMAN UNCONSCIOUS...
STILL CONSCIOUS, SOMEWHERE IN THERE, BUT WITH NO WILL OF HER OWN...
INDEED?! INTERESTING!
I WILL FOCUS MY BRAIN.
...IF YOU DON'T HAVE TO TAKE PART, THEN PERHAPS WE COULD CONTINUE THIS IN PRIVATE...
WHY DO YOU KEEP SAYING THAT?
THIS IS HELL.
LOOK AT WHAT'S IN FRONT OF US.
THEY'VE TAKEN SOMETHING WHICH USED TO BE ABOUT SCIENCE AND ADVENTURE AND MAGIC AND ROMANCE...
AND MADE PEOPLE SUBMIT TO THE POINT WHERE IT'S ALL ABOUT WHAT THIS ONE GUY WANTS--
ARE YOU... TALKING ABOUT OSBORN?
WHAT? NO!

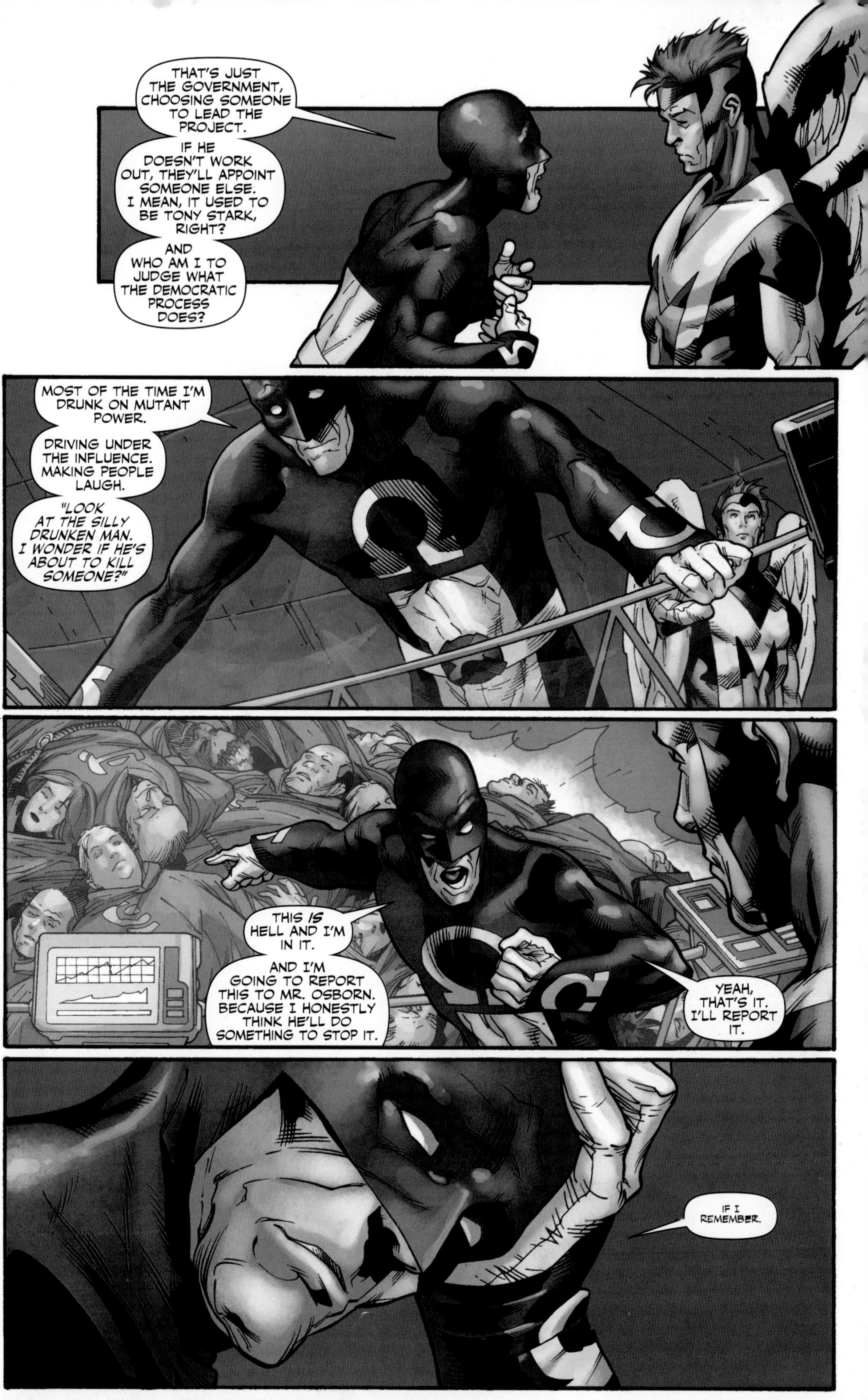
THAT'S JUST THE GOVERNMENT, CHOOSING SOMEONE TO LEAD THE PROJECT.
IF HE DOESN'T WORK OUT, THEY'LL APPOINT SOMEONE ELSE. I MEAN, IT USED TO BE TONY STARK, RIGHT?
AND WHO AM I TO JUDGE WHAT THE DEMOCRATIC PROCESS DOES?
MOST OF THE TIME I'M DRUNK ON MUTANT POWER.
DRIVING UNDER THE INFLUENCE. MAKING PEOPLE LAUGH.
"LOOK AT THE SILLY DRUNKEN MAN. I WONDER IF HE'S ABOUT TO KILL SOMEONE?"
THIS *IS* HELL AND I'M IN IT.
AND I'M GOING TO REPORT THIS TO MR. OSBORN. BECAUSE I HONESTLY THINK HE'LL DO SOMETHING TO STOP IT.
YEAH, THAT'S IT. I'LL REPORT IT.
IF I REMEMBER.

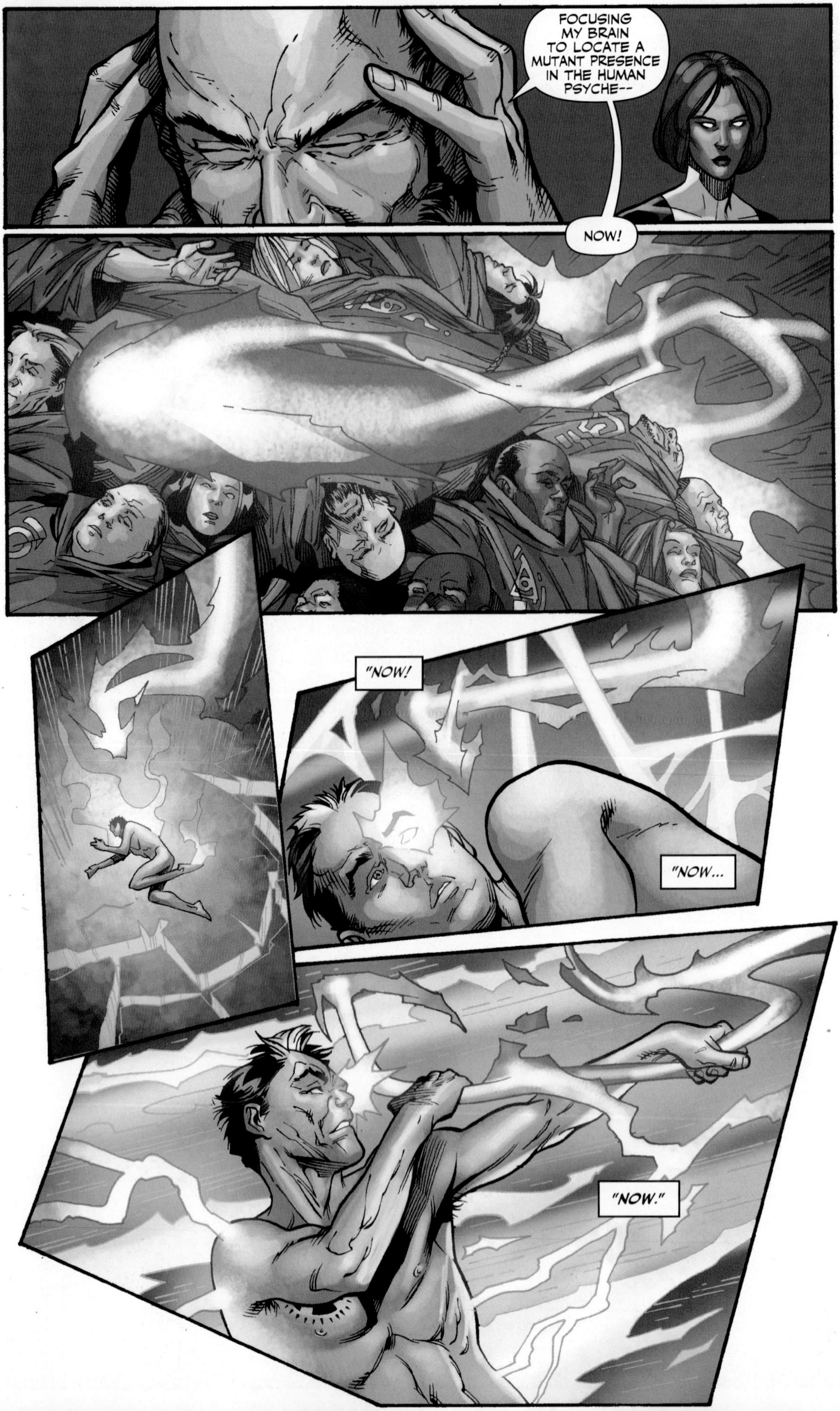
FOCUSING MY BRAIN TO LOCATE A MUTANT PRESENCE IN THE HUMAN PSYCHE--
NOW!
"NOW!
"NOW...
"NOW."

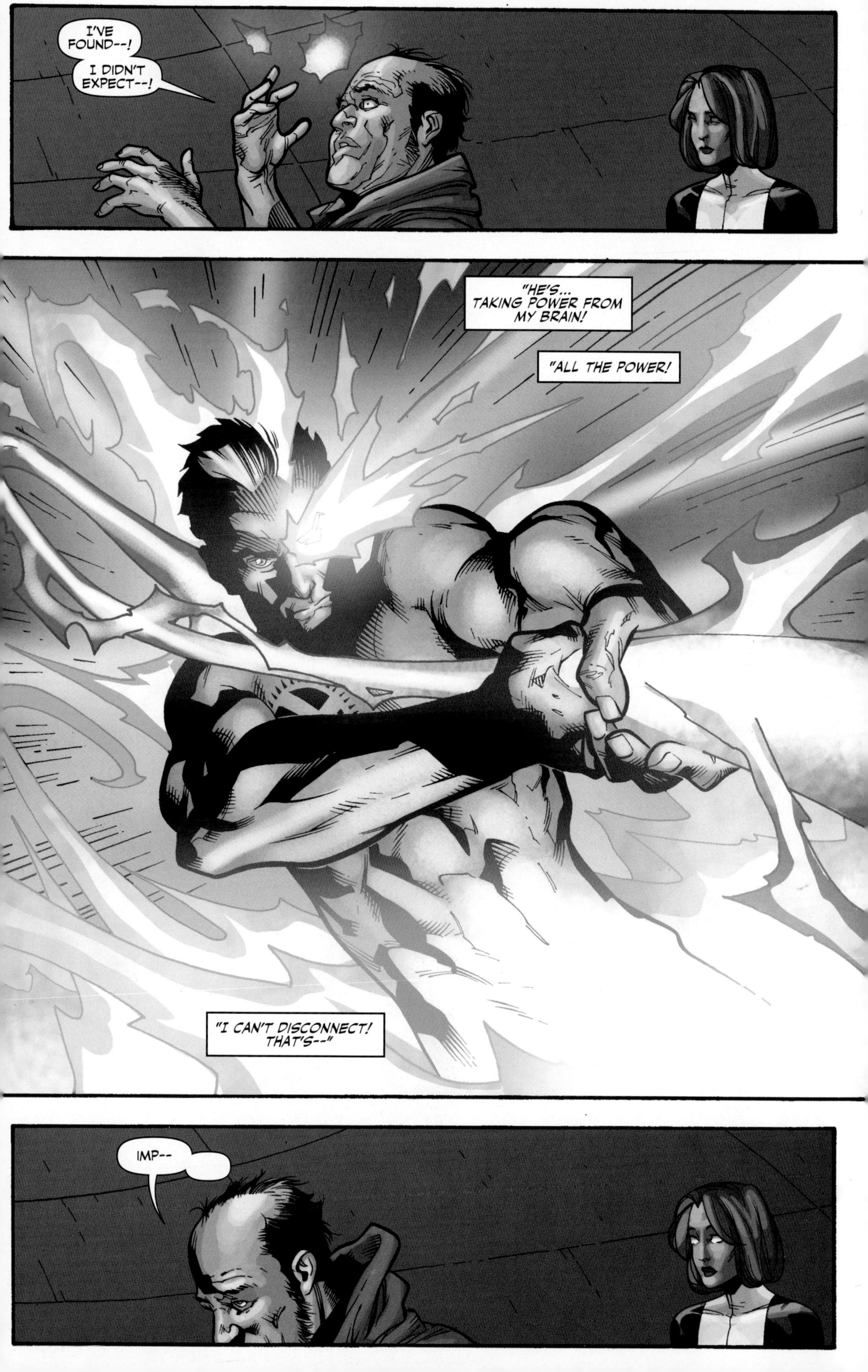
I'VE FOUND--!
I DIDN'T EXPECT--!
"HE'S... TAKING POWER FROM MY BRAIN!
"ALL THE POWER!
"I CAN'T DISCONNECT! THAT'S--"
IMP--

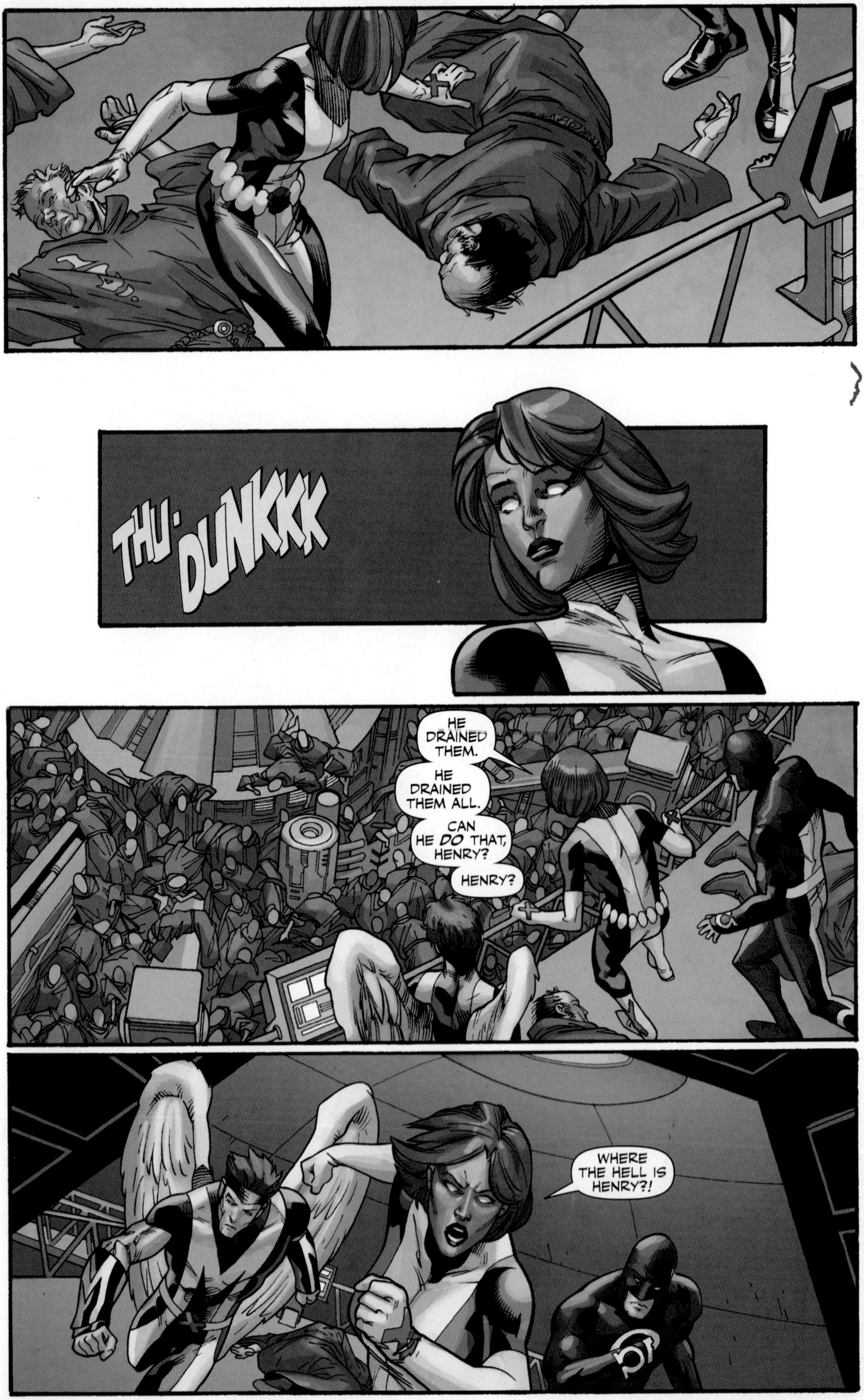
THU-DUNKKK
HE DRAINED THEM.
HE DRAINED THEM ALL.
CAN HE DO THAT, HENRY?
HENRY?
WHERE THE HELL IS HENRY?!

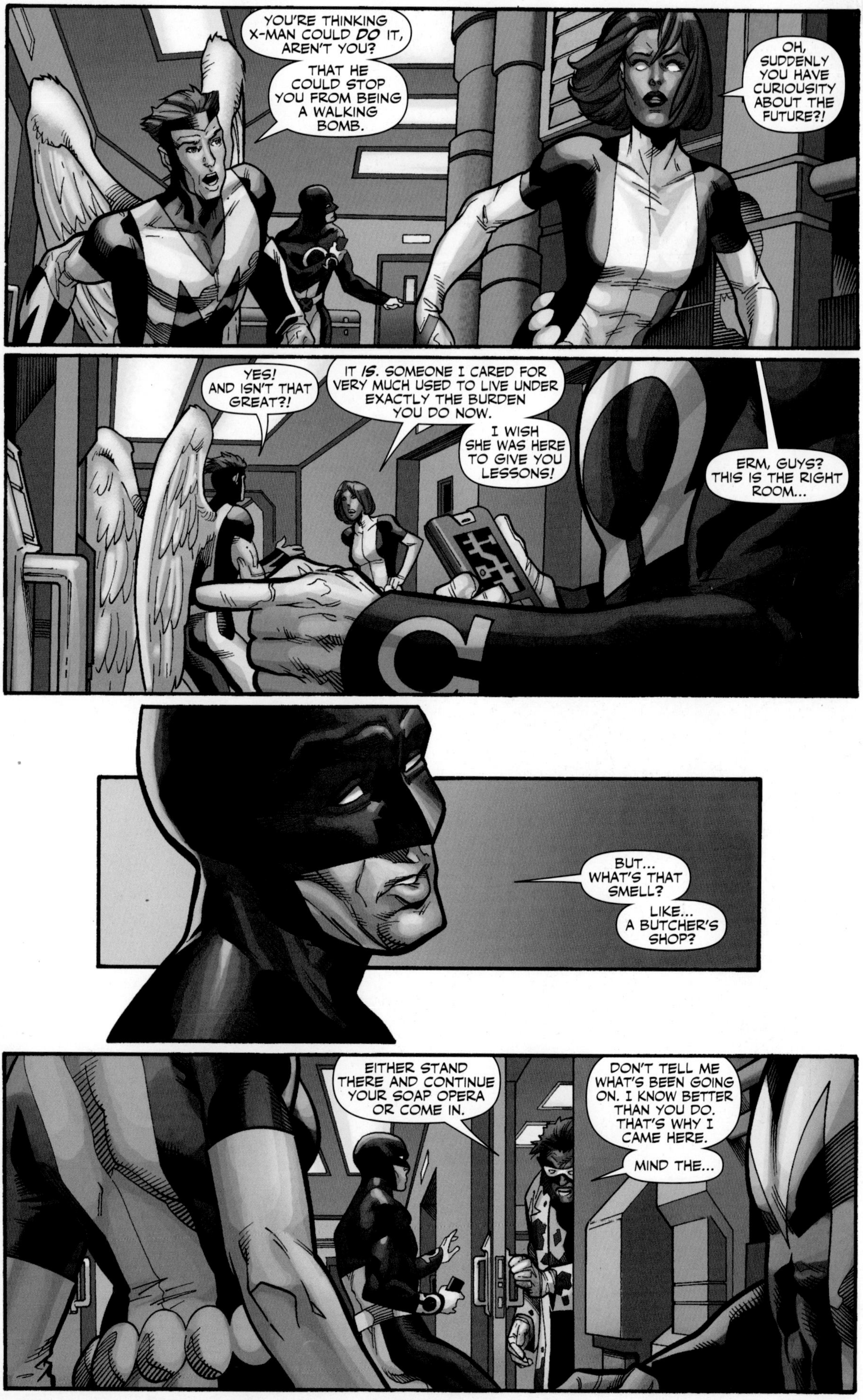
YOU'RE THINKING X-MAN COULD *DO* IT, AREN'T YOU?
THAT HE COULD STOP YOU FROM BEING A WALKING BOMB.
OH, SUDDENLY YOU HAVE CURIOUSITY ABOUT THE FUTURE?!
YES! AND ISN'T THAT GREAT?!
IT *IS*. SOMEONE I CARED FOR VERY MUCH USED TO LIVE UNDER EXACTLY THE BURDEN YOU DO NOW.
I WISH SHE WAS HERE TO GIVE YOU LESSONS!
ERM, GUYS? THIS IS THE RIGHT ROOM...
BUT... WHAT'S THAT SMELL?
LIKE... A BUTCHER'S SHOP?
EITHER STAND THERE AND CONTINUE YOUR SOAP OPERA OR COME IN.
DON'T TELL ME WHAT'S BEEN GOING ON. I KNOW BETTER THAN YOU DO. THAT'S WHY I CAME HERE.
MIND THE...

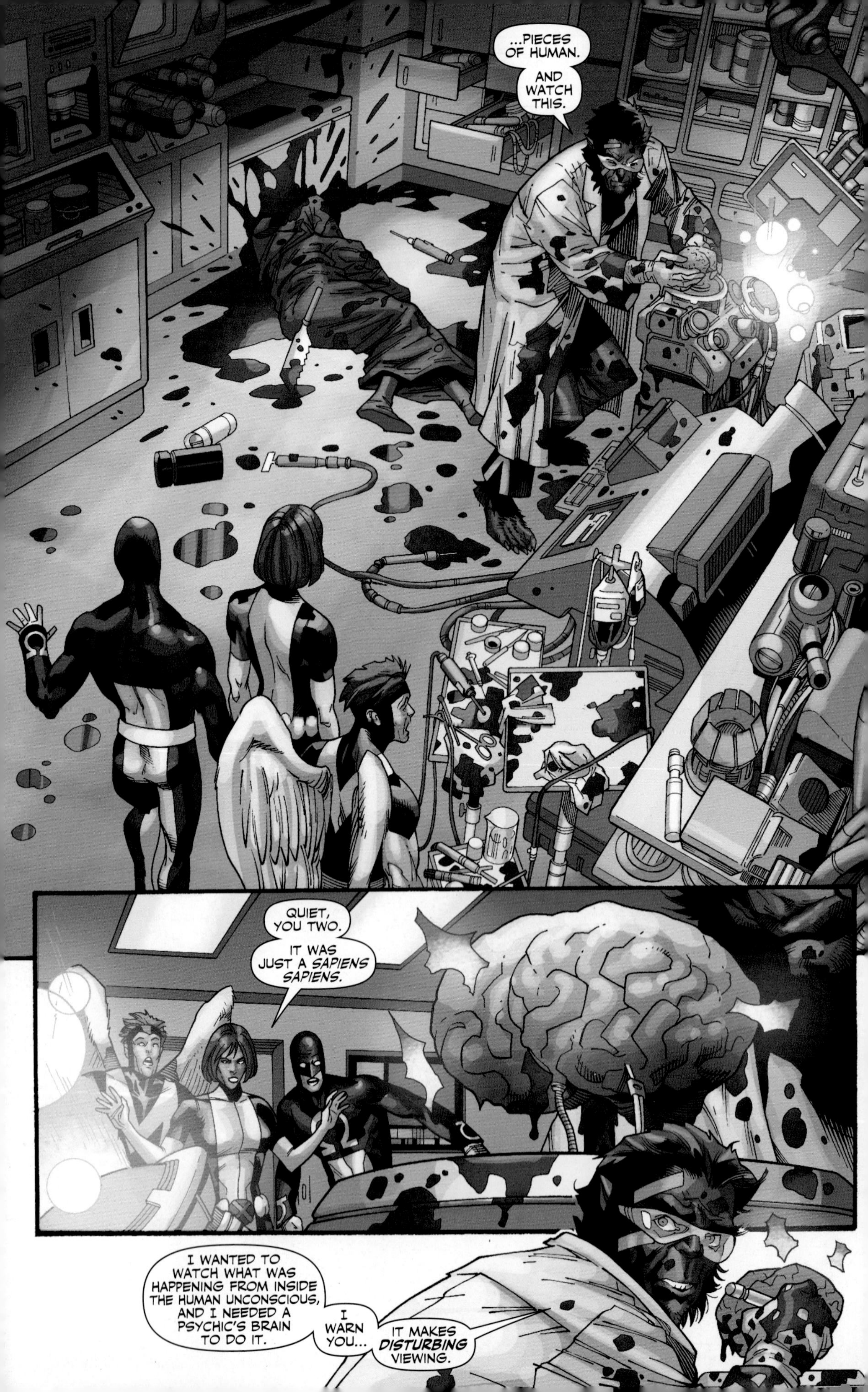
...PIECES OF HUMAN.
AND WATCH THIS.
QUIET, YOU TWO.
IT WAS JUST A SAPIENS SAPIENS.
I WANTED TO WATCH WHAT WAS HAPPENING FROM INSIDE THE HUMAN UNCONSCIOUS, AND I NEEDED A PSYCHIC'S BRAIN TO DO IT.
I WARN YOU...
IT MAKES DISTURBING VIEWING.

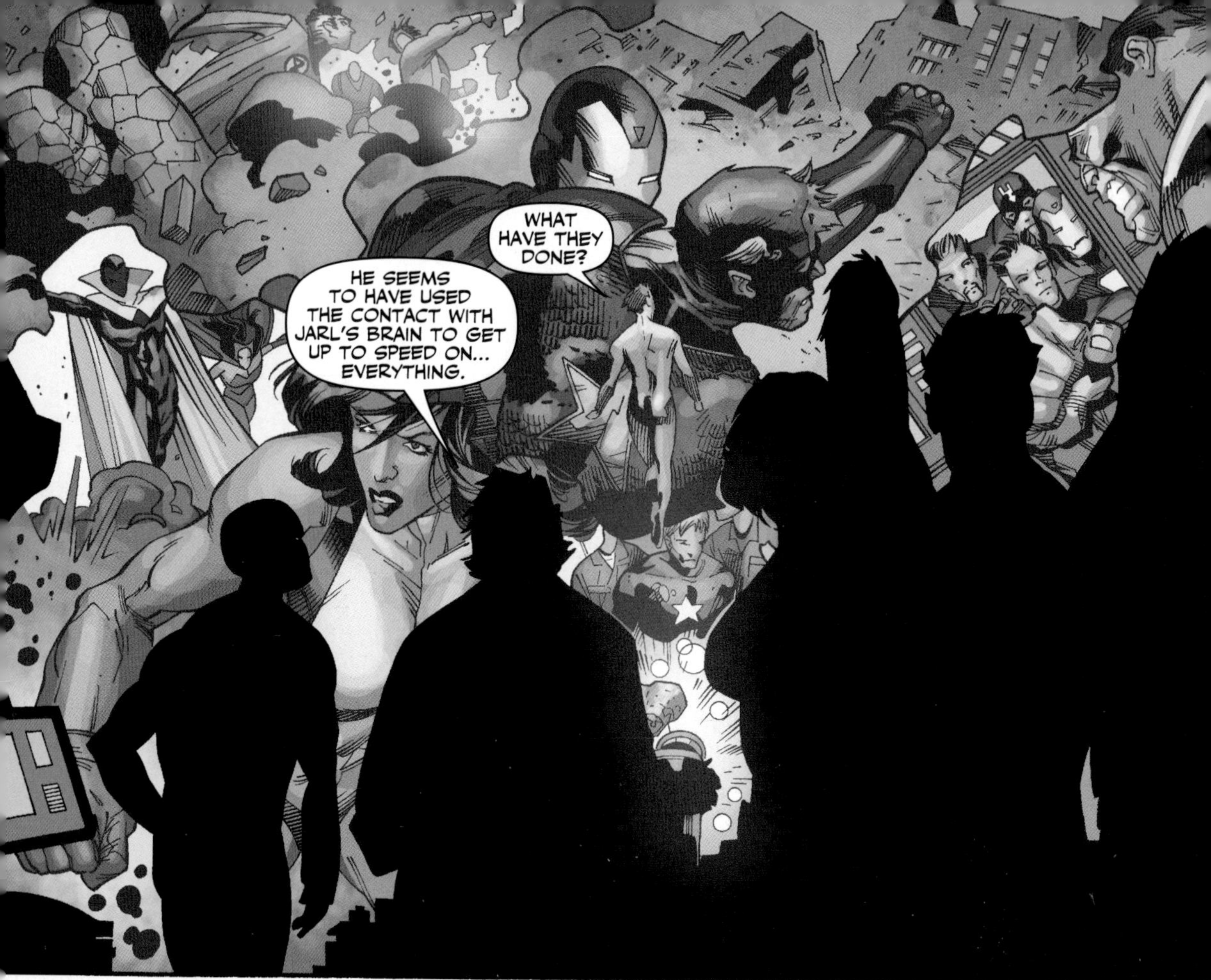
HE SEEMS TO HAVE USED THE CONTACT WITH JARL'S BRAIN TO GET UP TO SPEED ON... EVERYTHING.
WHAT HAVE THEY DONE?
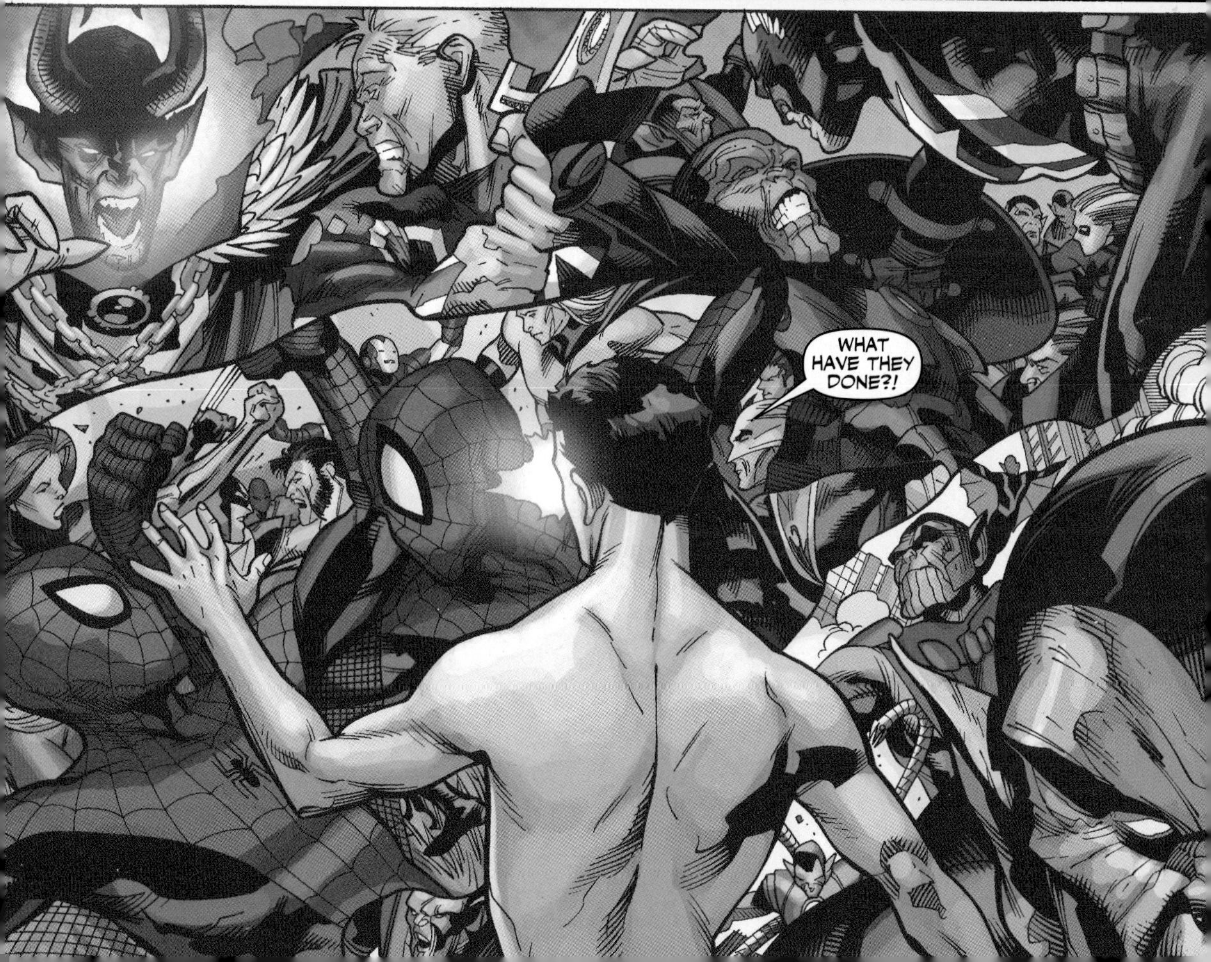
WHAT HAVE THEY DONE?!

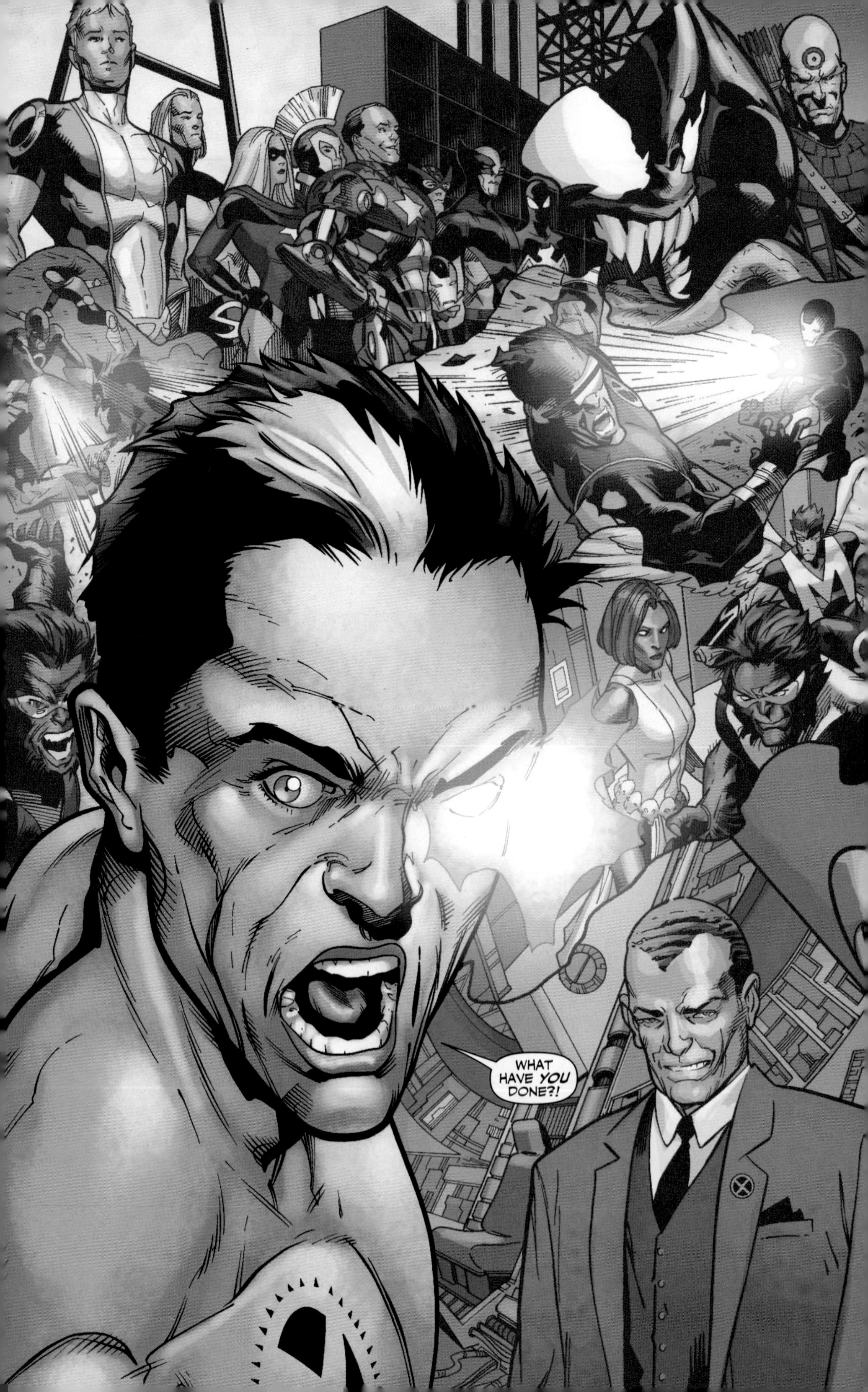
WHAT HAVE YOU DONE?!

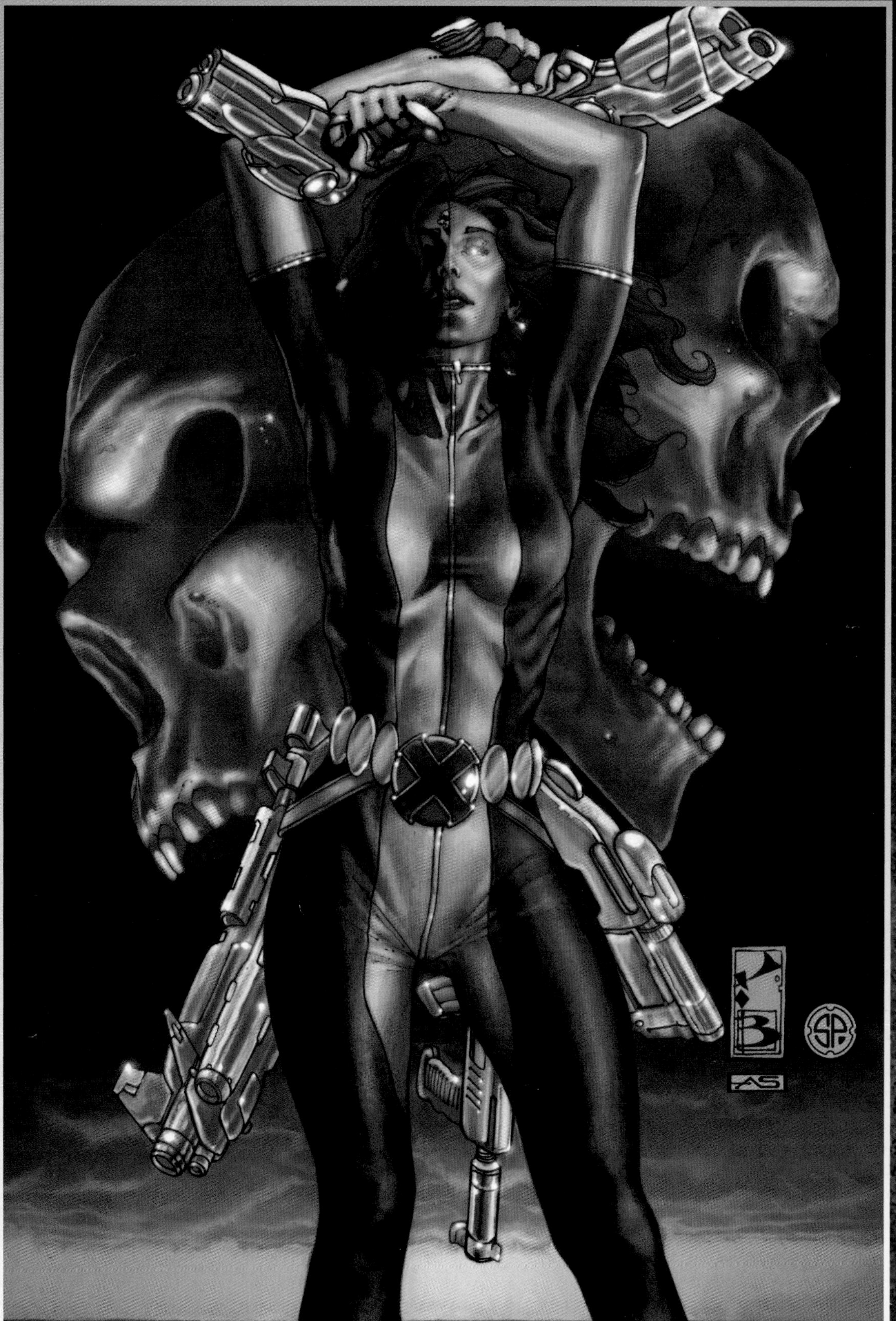
AS

3

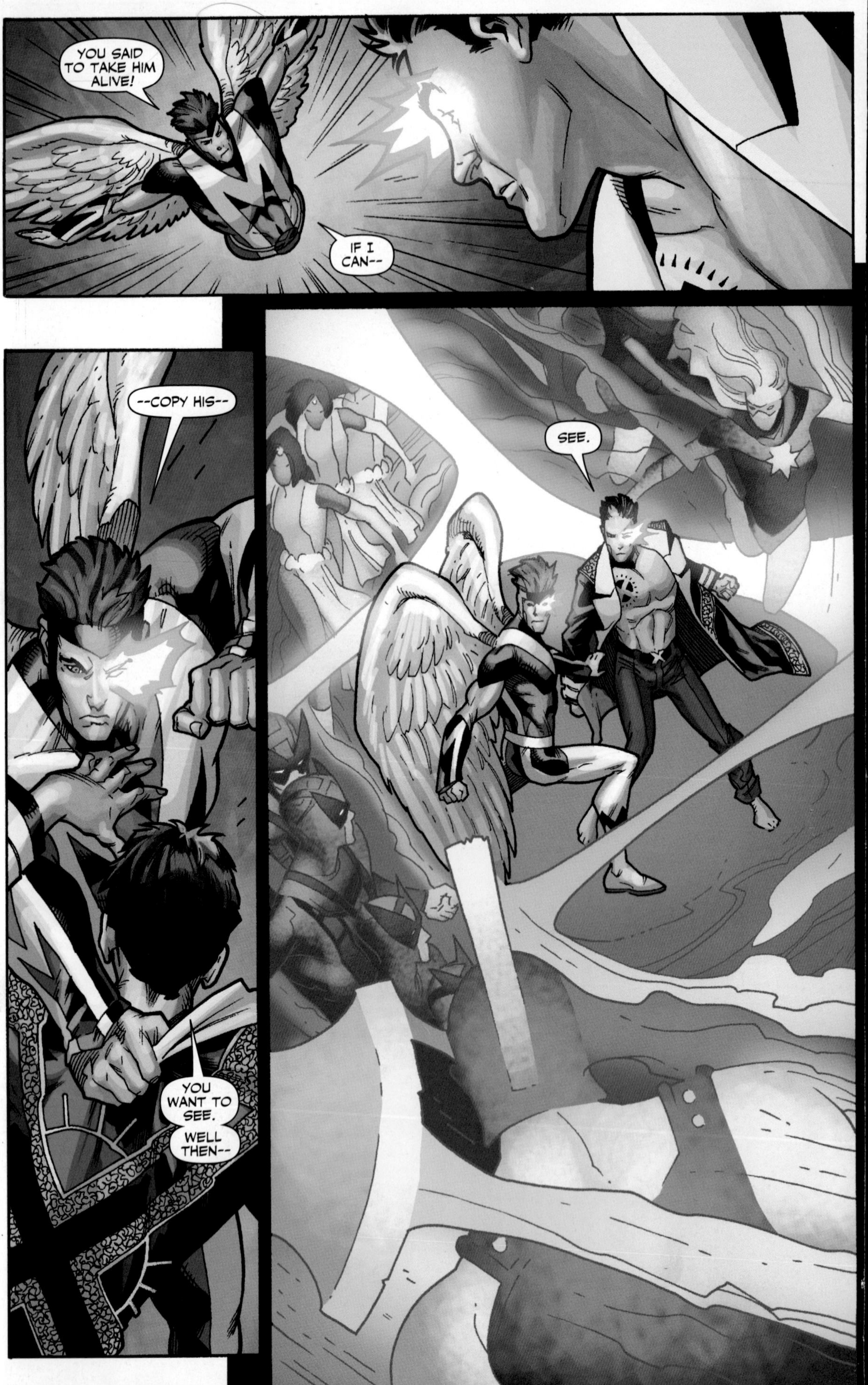
YOU SAID TO TAKE HIM ALIVE!
IF I CAN--
--COPY HIS--
YOU WANT TO SEE.
WELL THEN--
SEE.

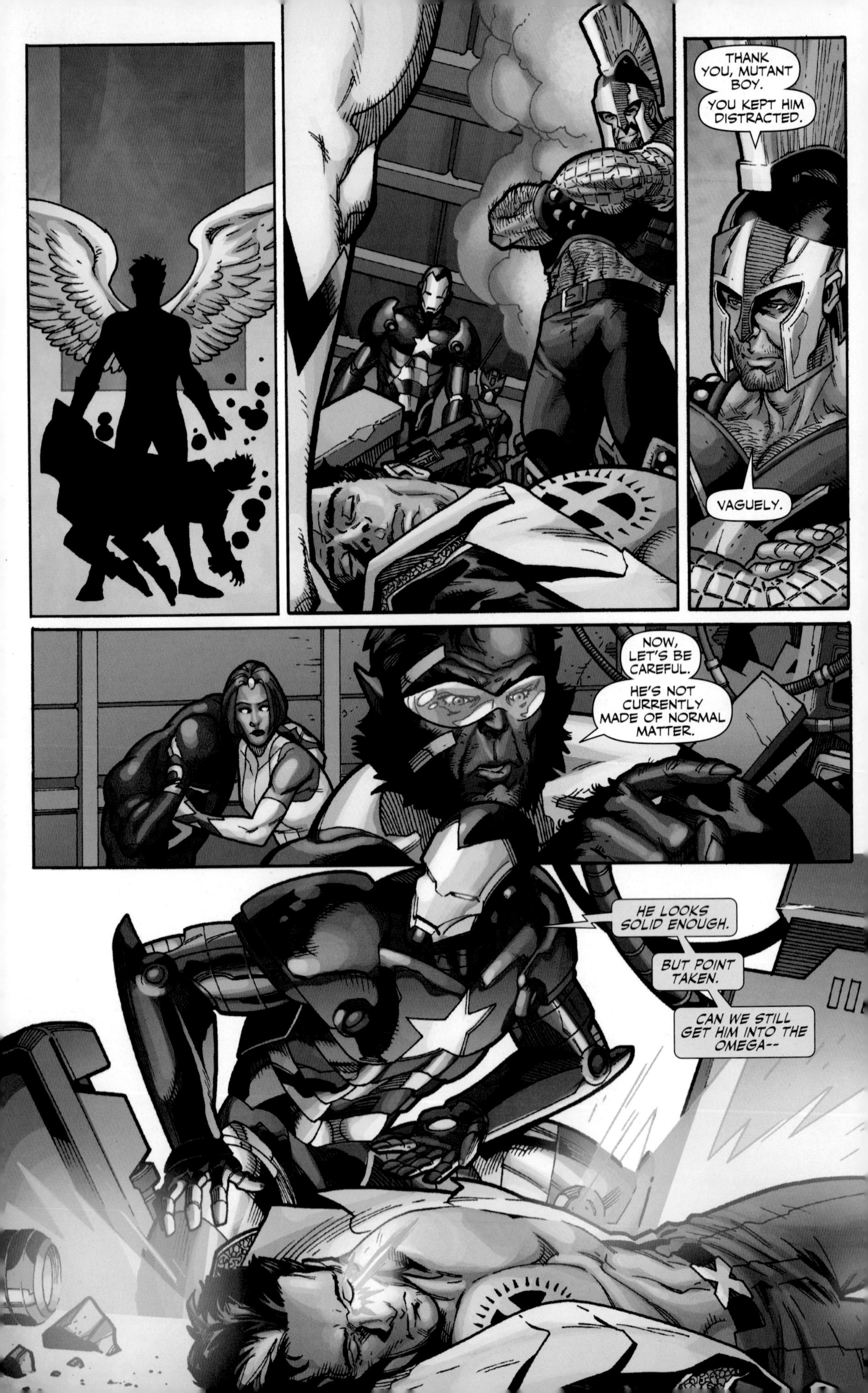
THANK YOU, MUTANT BOY.
YOU KEPT HIM DISTRACTED.
VAGUELY.
NOW, LET'S BE CAREFUL.
HE'S NOT CURRENTLY MADE OF NORMAL MATTER.
HE LOOKS SOLID ENOUGH.
BUT POINT TAKEN.
CAN WE STILL GET HIM INTO THE OMEGA--

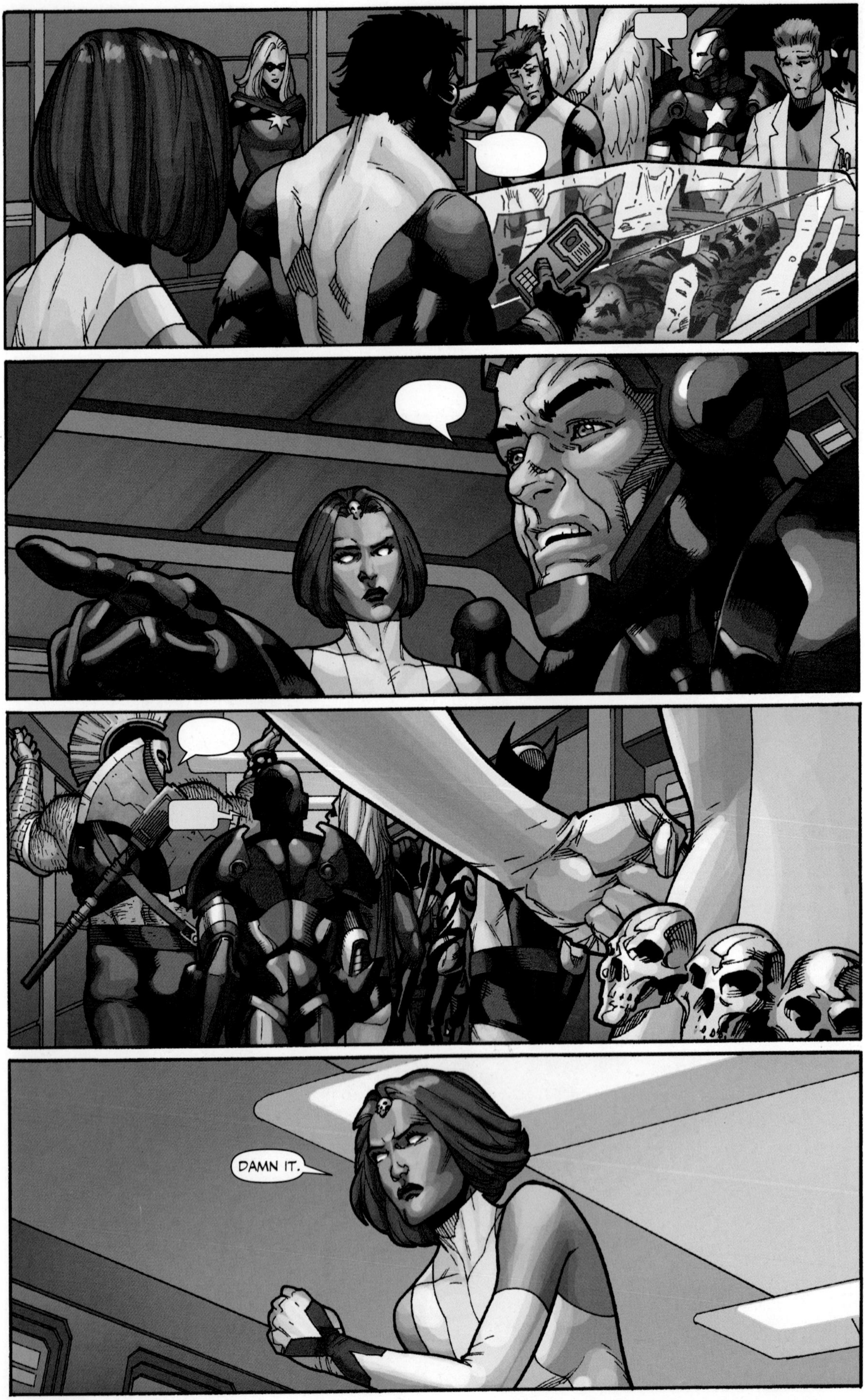
DAMN IT.

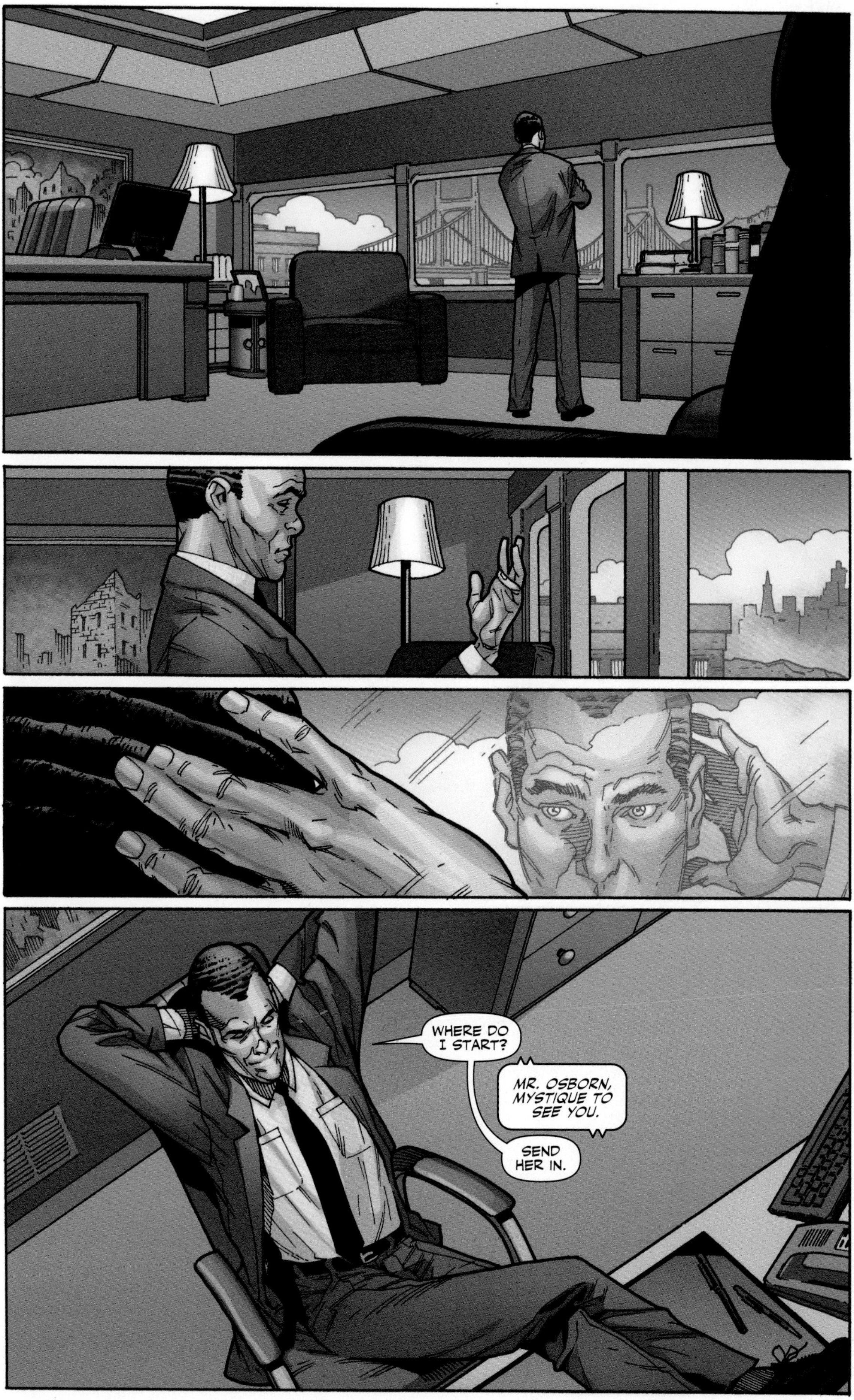
WHERE DO I START?
MR. OSBORN, MYSTIQUE TO SEE YOU.
SEND HER IN.

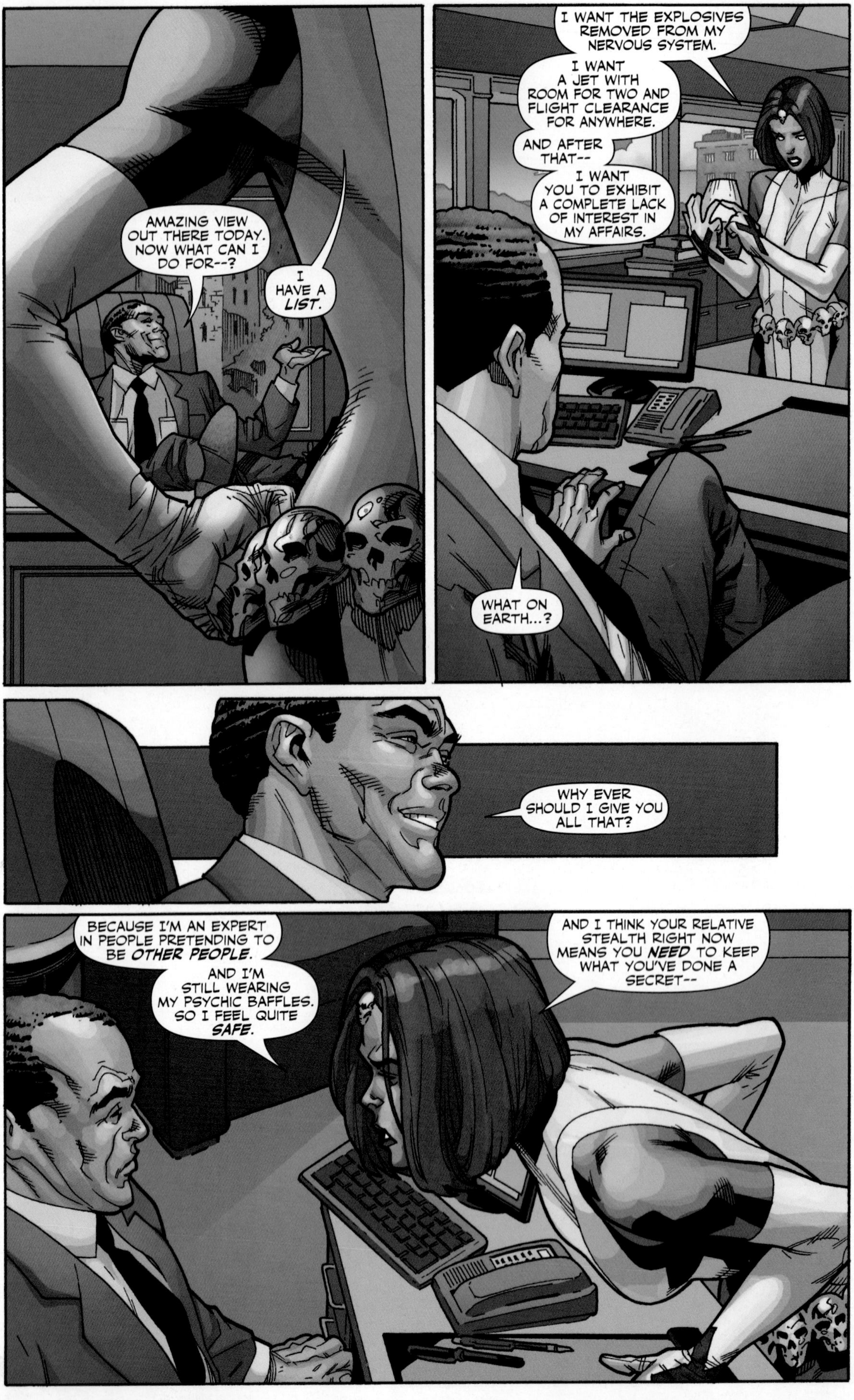
AMAZING VIEW OUT THERE TODAY. NOW WHAT CAN I DO FOR--?
I HAVE A *LIST*.
I WANT THE EXPLOSIVES REMOVED FROM MY NERVOUS SYSTEM.
I WANT A JET WITH ROOM FOR TWO AND FLIGHT CLEARANCE FOR ANYWHERE.
AND AFTER THAT--
I WANT YOU TO EXHIBIT A COMPLETE LACK OF INTEREST IN MY AFFAIRS.
WHAT ON EARTH...?
WHY EVER SHOULD I GIVE YOU ALL THAT?
BECAUSE I'M AN EXPERT IN PEOPLE PRETENDING TO BE *OTHER PEOPLE*.
AND I'M STILL WEARING MY PSYCHIC BAFFLES. SO I FEEL QUITE *SAFE*.
AND I THINK YOUR RELATIVE STEALTH RIGHT NOW MEANS YOU *NEED* TO KEEP WHAT YOU'VE DONE A SECRET--

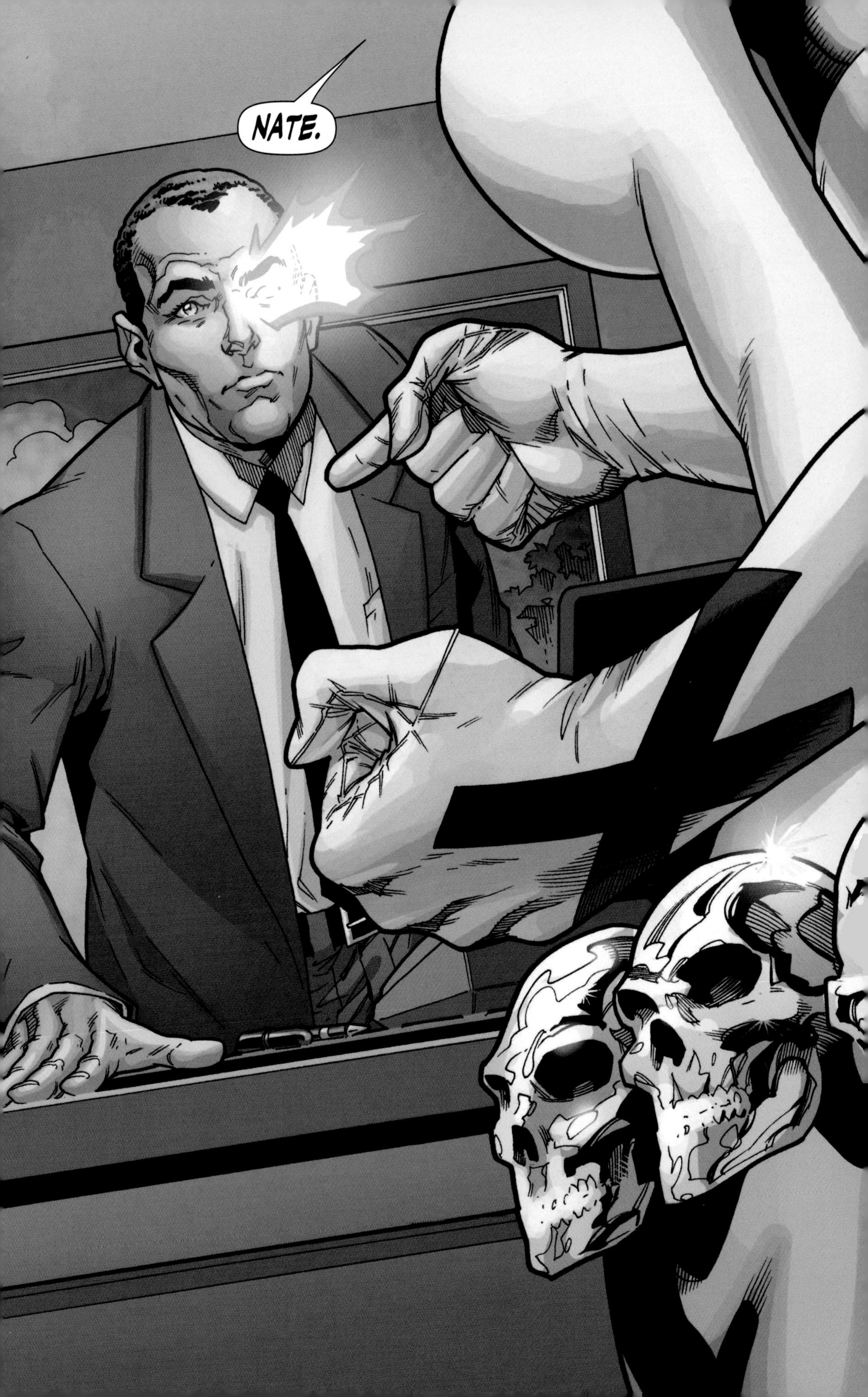
NATE.

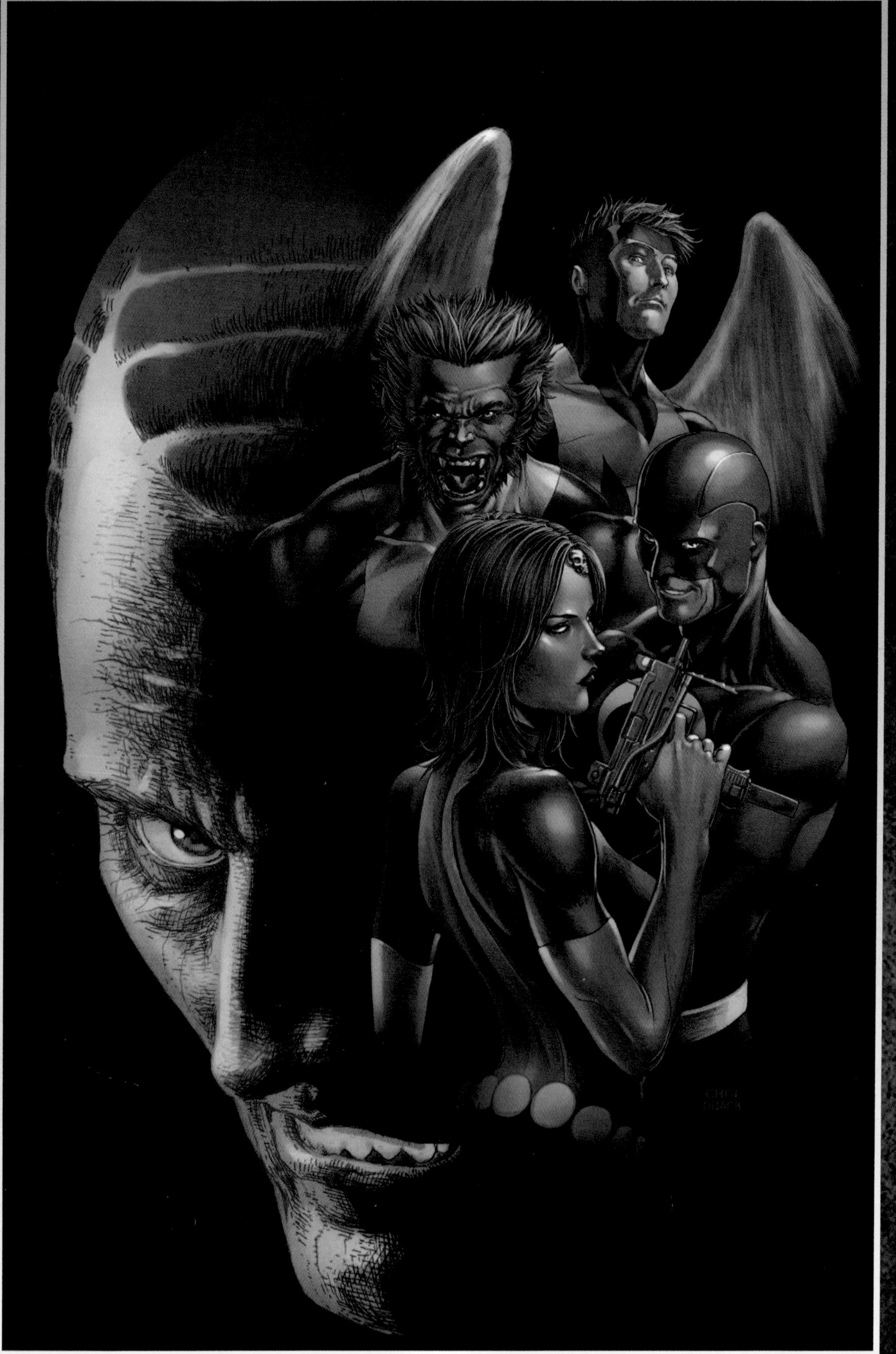

4

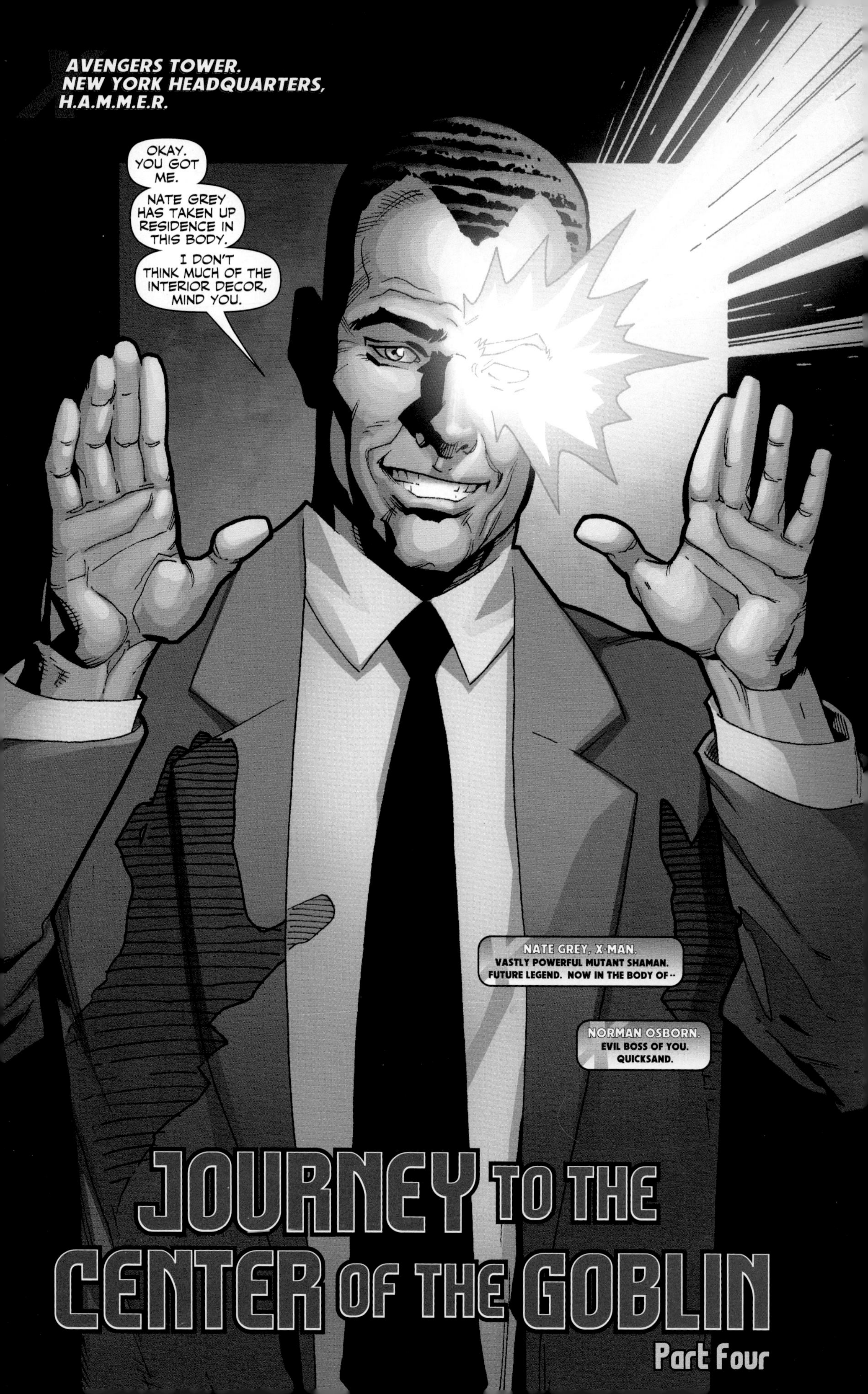
AVENGERS TOWER. NEW YORK HEADQUARTERS, H.A.M.M.E.R.
OKAY. YOU GOT ME.
NATE GREY HAS TAKEN UP RESIDENCE IN THIS BODY.
I DON'T THINK MUCH OF THE INTERIOR DECOR, MIND YOU.
NATE GREY, X-MAN. VASTLY POWERFUL MUTANT SHAMAN. FUTURE LEGEND. NOW IN THE BODY OF--
NORMAN OSBORN. EVIL BOSS OF YOU. QUICKSAND.
JOURNEY TO THE CENTER OF THE GOBLIN
Part Four

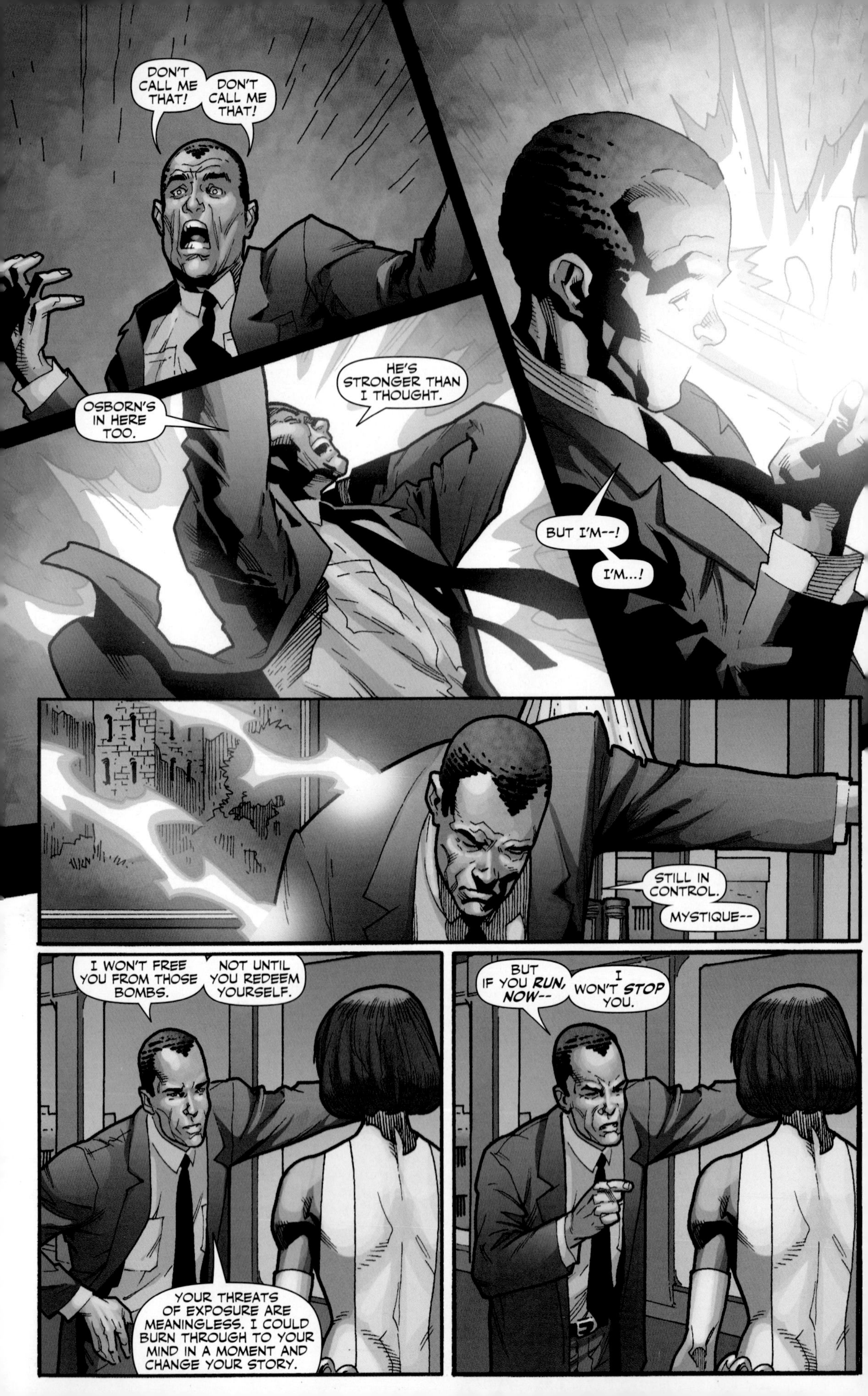
DON'T CALL ME THAT!
DON'T CALL ME THAT!
HE'S STRONGER THAN I THOUGHT.
OSBORN'S IN HERE TOO.
BUT I'M--!
I'M...!
STILL IN CONTROL.
MYSTIQUE--
I WON'T FREE YOU FROM THOSE BOMBS.
NOT UNTIL YOU REDEEM YOURSELF.
YOUR THREATS OF EXPOSURE ARE MEANINGLESS. I COULD BURN THROUGH TO YOUR MIND IN A MOMENT AND CHANGE YOUR STORY.
BUT IF YOU *RUN, NOW*--
I WON'T *STOP* YOU.

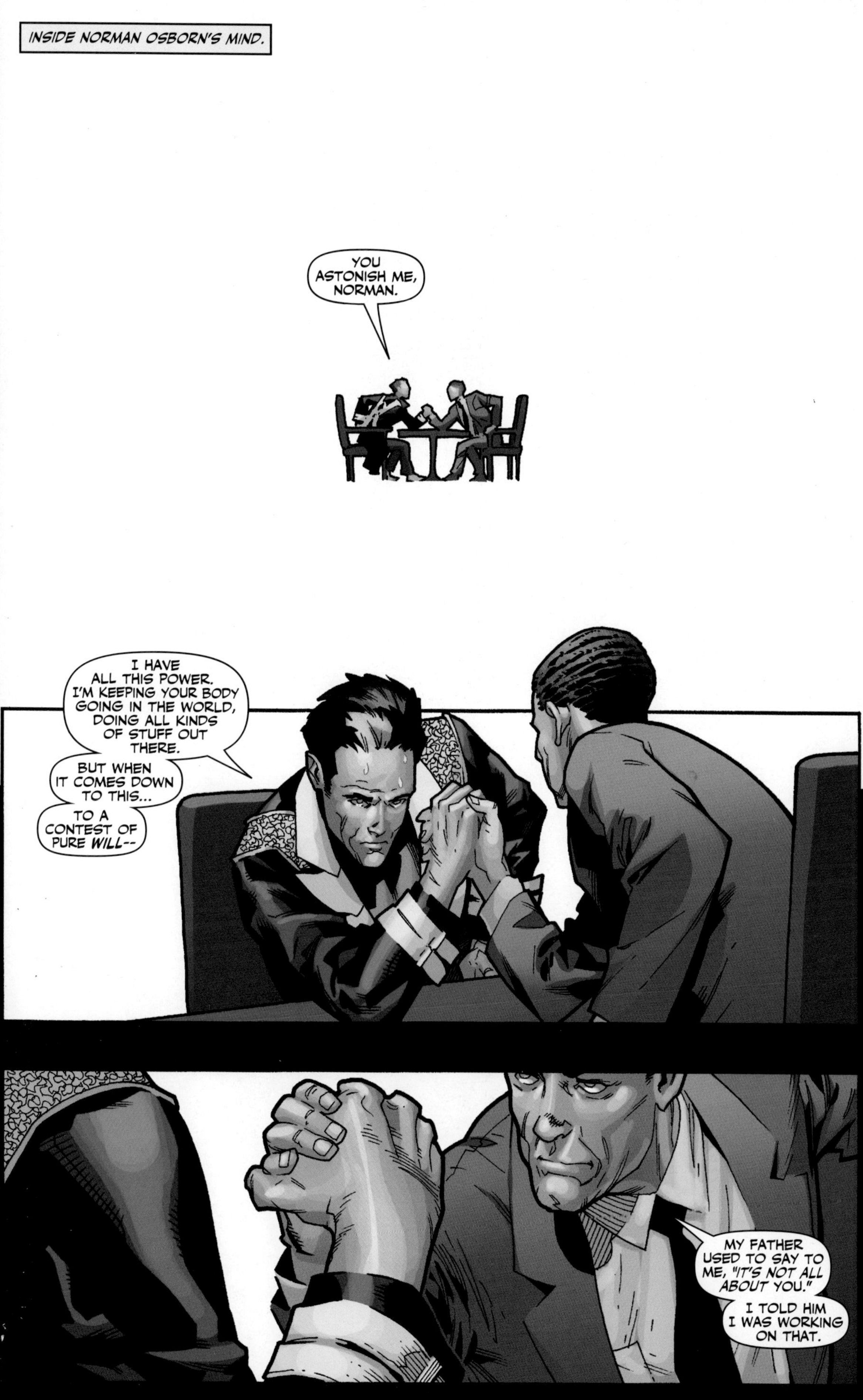
INSIDE NORMAN OSBORN'S MIND.
YOU ASTONISH ME, NORMAN.
I HAVE ALL THIS POWER. I'M KEEPING YOUR BODY GOING IN THE WORLD, DOING ALL KINDS OF STUFF OUT THERE.
BUT WHEN IT COMES DOWN TO THIS...
TO A CONTEST OF PURE *WILL*--
MY FATHER USED TO SAY TO ME, *"IT'S NOT ALL ABOUT YOU."*
I TOLD HIM I WAS WORKING ON THAT.

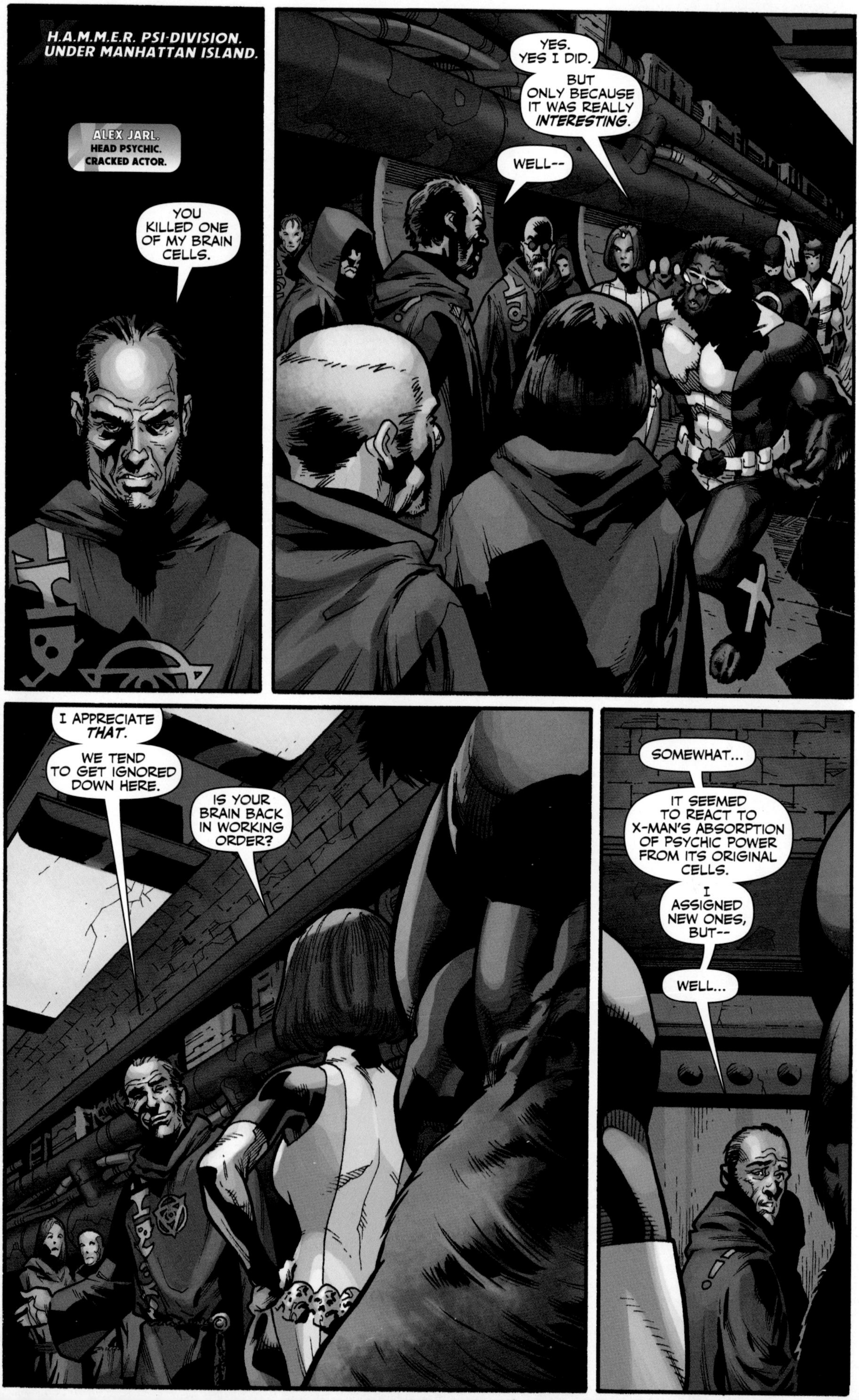
H.A.M.M.E.R. PSI-DIVISION. UNDER MANHATTAN ISLAND.
ALEX JARL. HEAD PSYCHIC. CRACKED ACTOR.
YOU KILLED ONE OF MY BRAIN CELLS.
YES. YES I DID.
BUT ONLY BECAUSE IT WAS REALLY *INTERESTING*.
WELL--
I APPRECIATE *THAT*.
WE TEND TO GET IGNORED DOWN HERE.
IS YOUR BRAIN BACK IN WORKING ORDER?
SOMEWHAT...
IT SEEMED TO REACT TO X-MAN'S ABSORPTION OF PSYCHIC POWER FROM ITS ORIGINAL CELLS.
I ASSIGNED NEW ONES, BUT--
WELL...

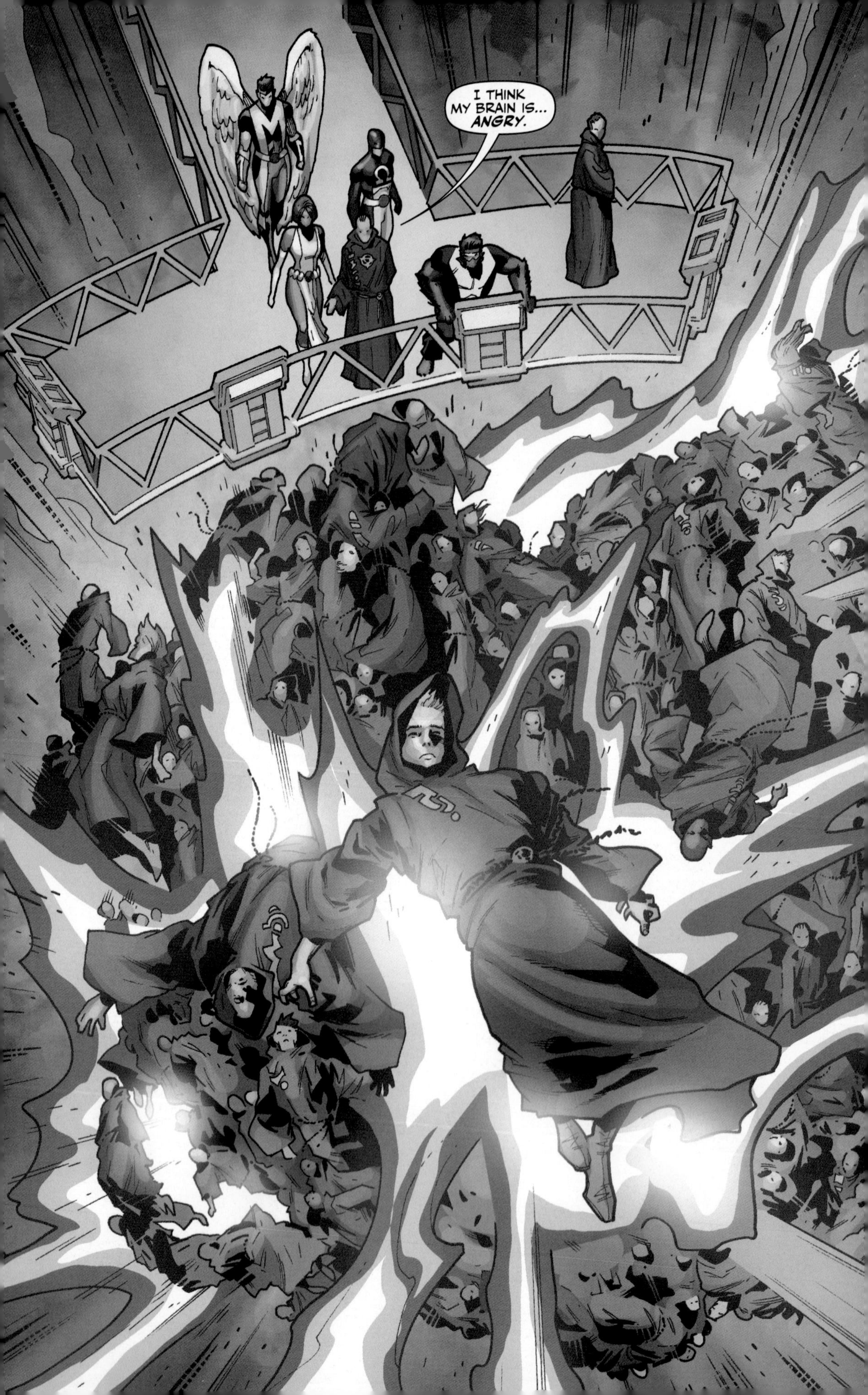
I THINK MY BRAIN IS... ANGRY.

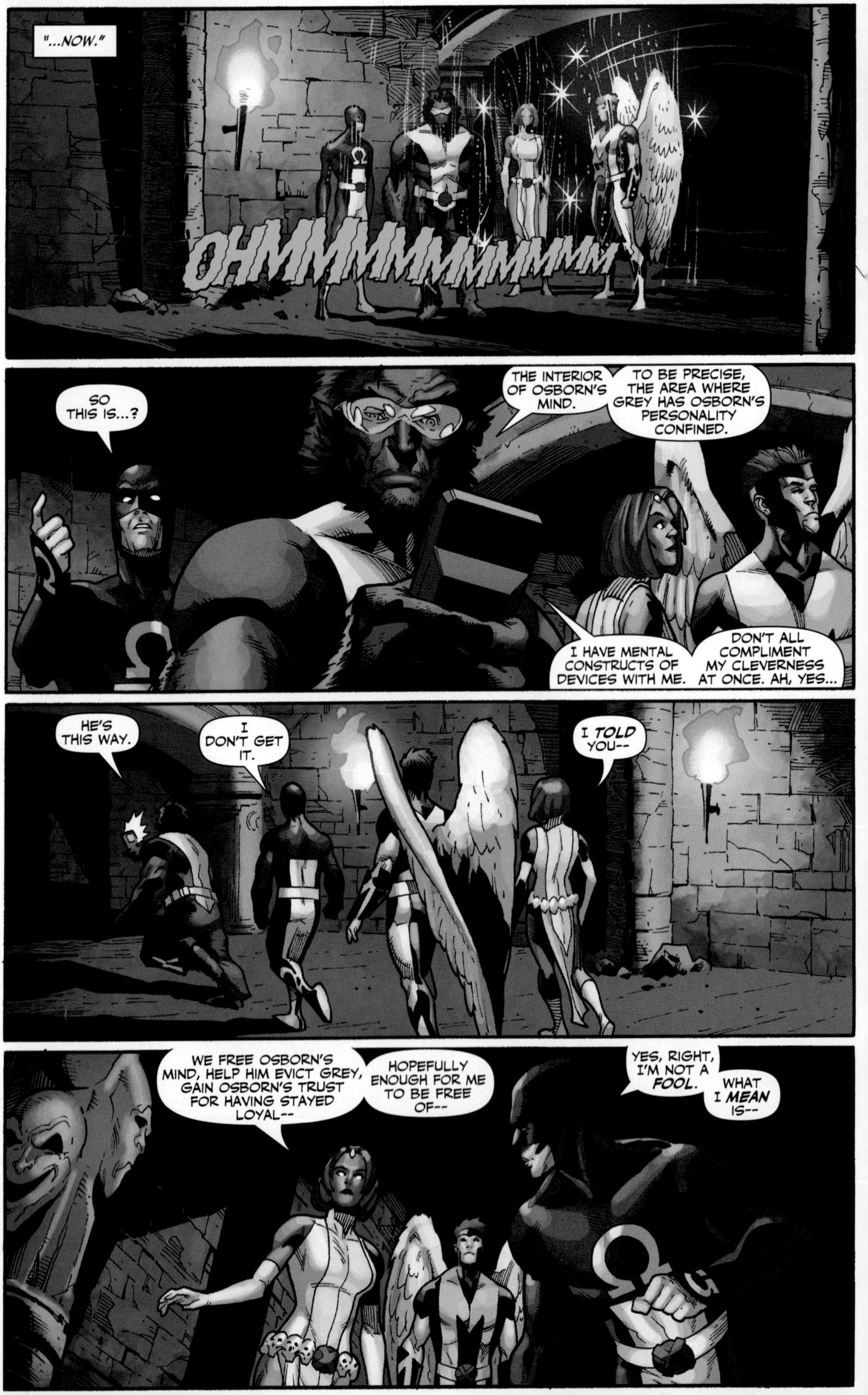
"...NOW."
OHMMMMMMMMMMM
SO THIS IS...?
THE INTERIOR OF OSBORN'S MIND.
TO BE PRECISE, THE AREA WHERE GREY HAS OSBORN'S PERSONALITY CONFINED.
I HAVE MENTAL CONSTRUCTS OF DEVICES WITH ME.
DON'T ALL COMPLIMENT MY CLEVERNESS AT ONCE. AH, YES...
HE'S THIS WAY.
I DON'T GET IT.
I TOLD YOU--
WE FREE OSBORN'S MIND, HELP HIM EVICT GREY, GAIN OSBORN'S TRUST FOR HAVING STAYED LOYAL--
HOPEFULLY ENOUGH FOR ME TO BE FREE OF--
YES, RIGHT, I'M NOT A FOOL.
WHAT I MEAN IS--

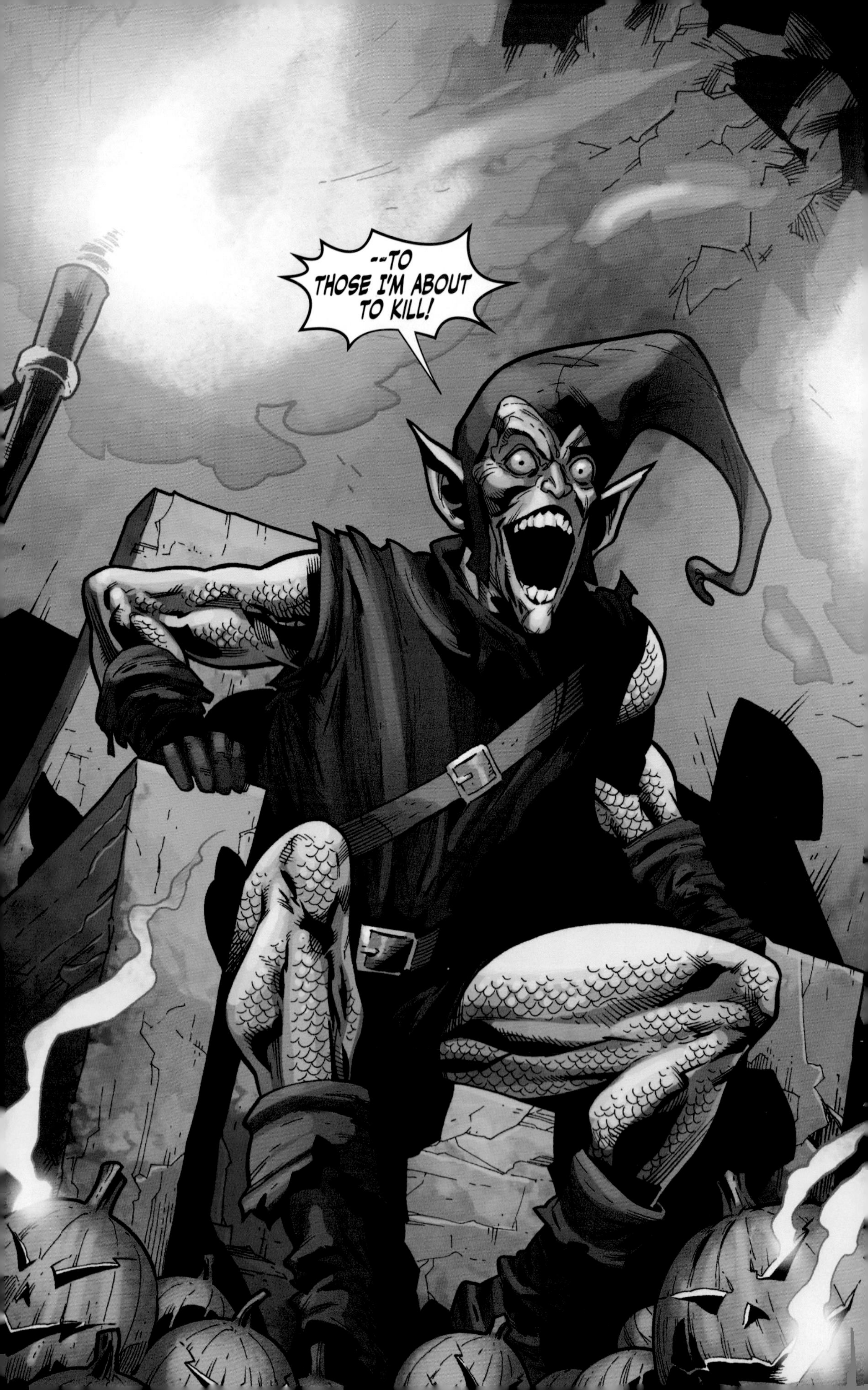
--TO THOSE I'M ABOUT TO KILL!

MYSTIQUE DESIGNS BY LEONARD KIRK

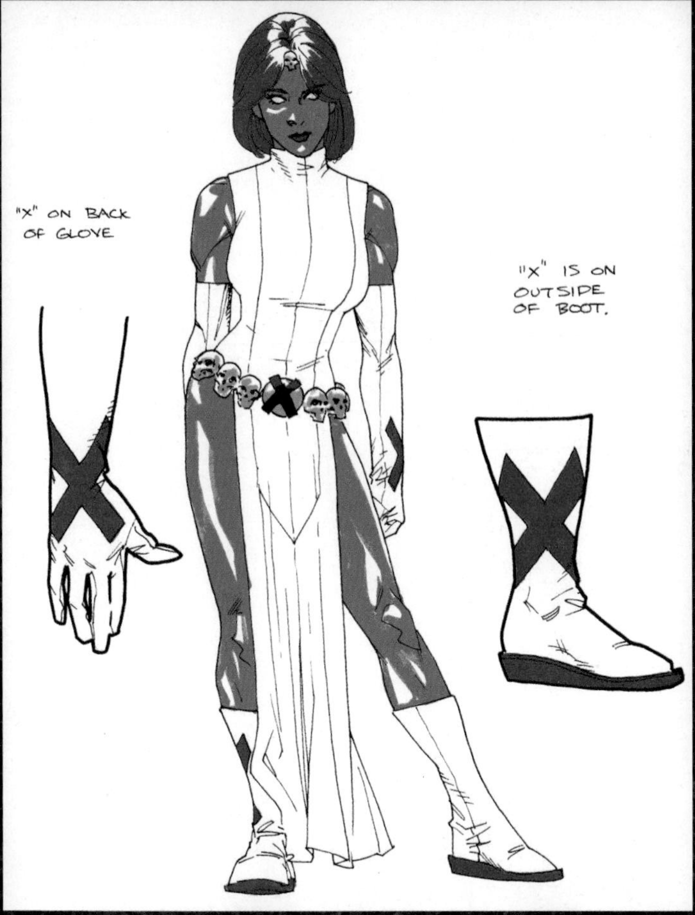

"X" ON BACK OF GLOVE
"X" IS ON OUTSIDE OF BOOT.

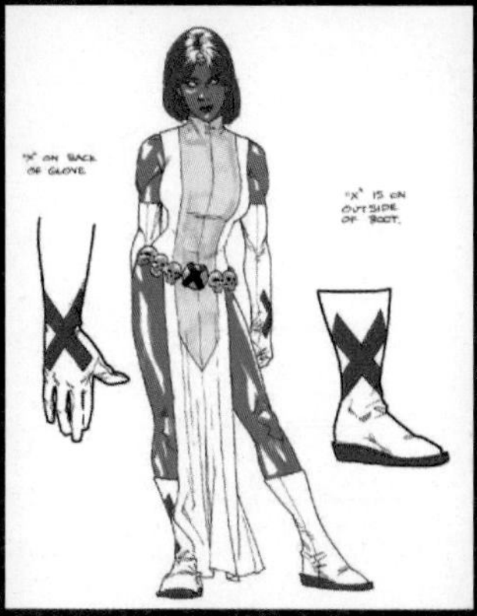

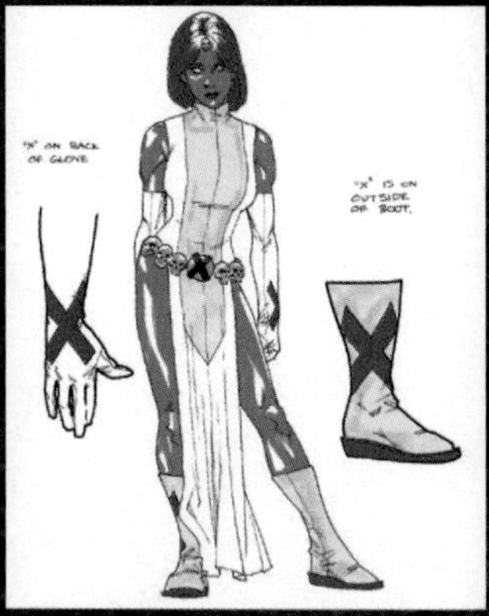

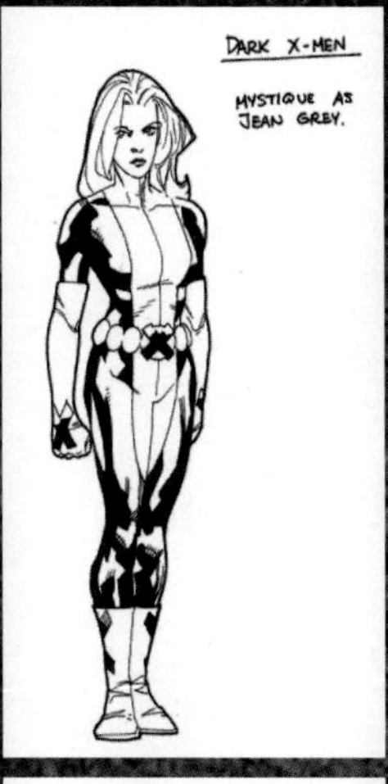

DARK X-MEN
MYSTIQUE AS JEAN GREY.

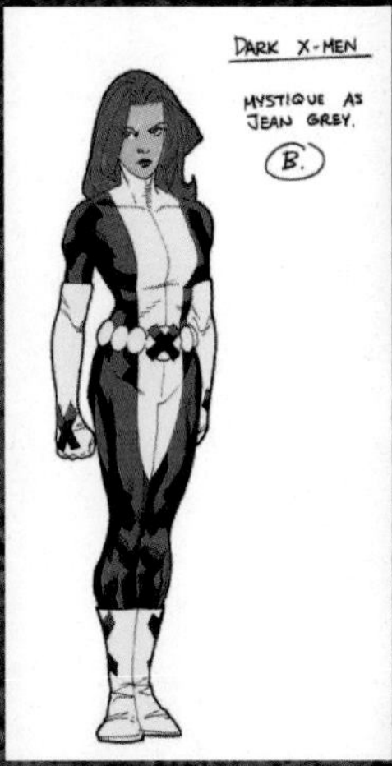

DARK X-MEN
MYSTIQUE AS JEAN GREY.
B.

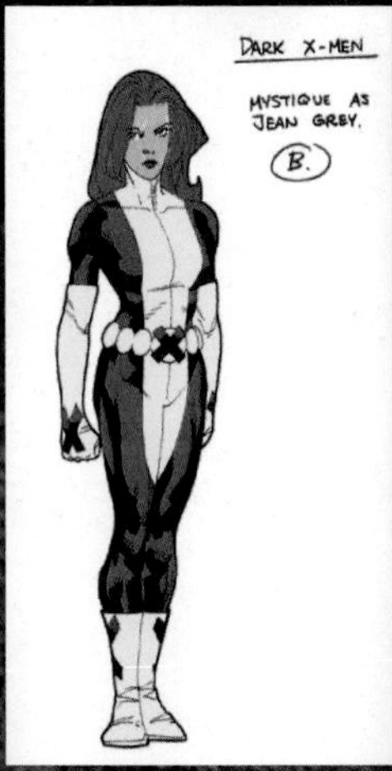

DARK X-MEN
MYSTIQUE AS JEAN GREY.
B.

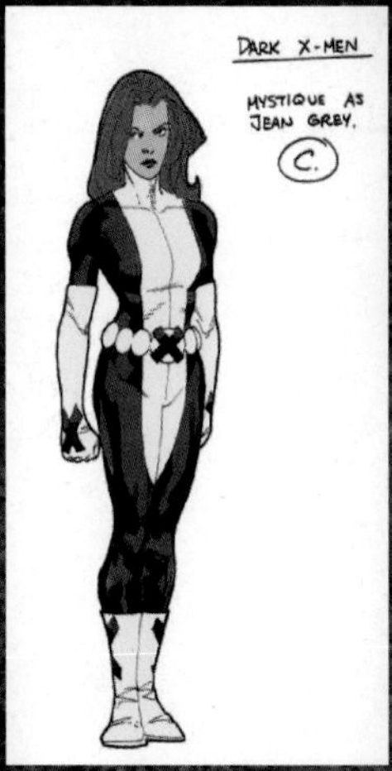

DARK X-MEN
MYSTIQUE AS JEAN GREY.
C.

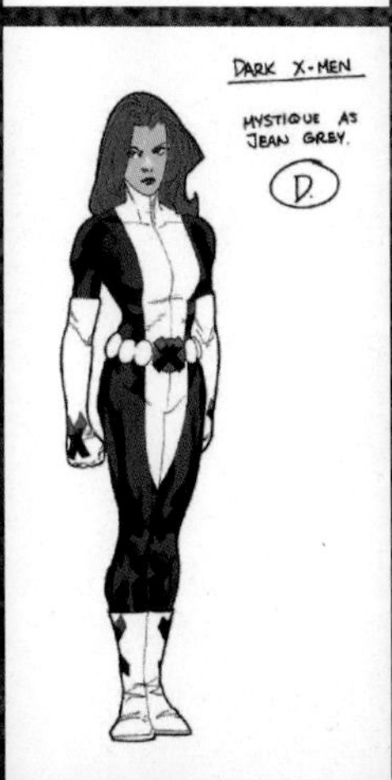

DARK X-MEN
MYSTIQUE AS JEAN GREY.
D.

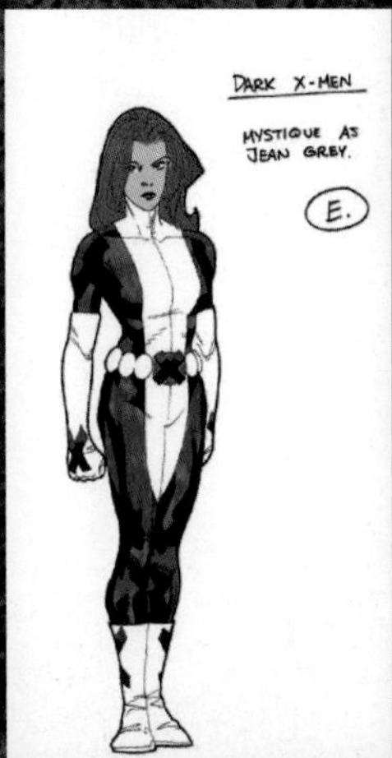

DARK X-MEN
MYSTIQUE AS JEAN GREY.
E.

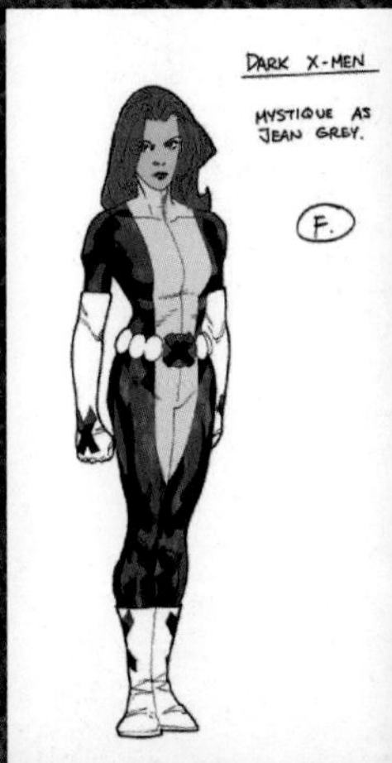

DARK X-MEN
MYSTIQUE AS JEAN GREY.
F.

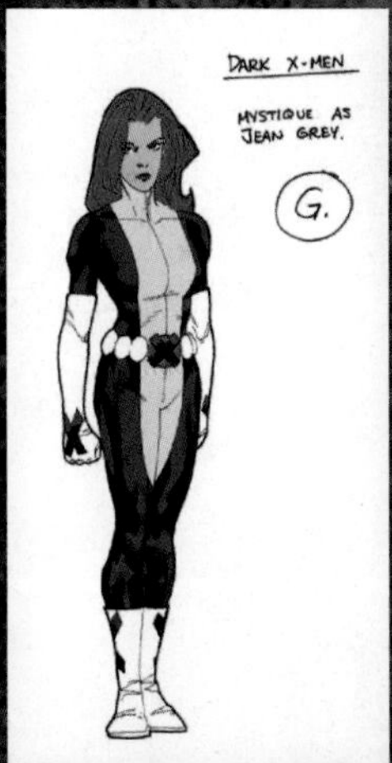

DARK X-MEN
MYSTIQUE AS JEAN GREY.
G.

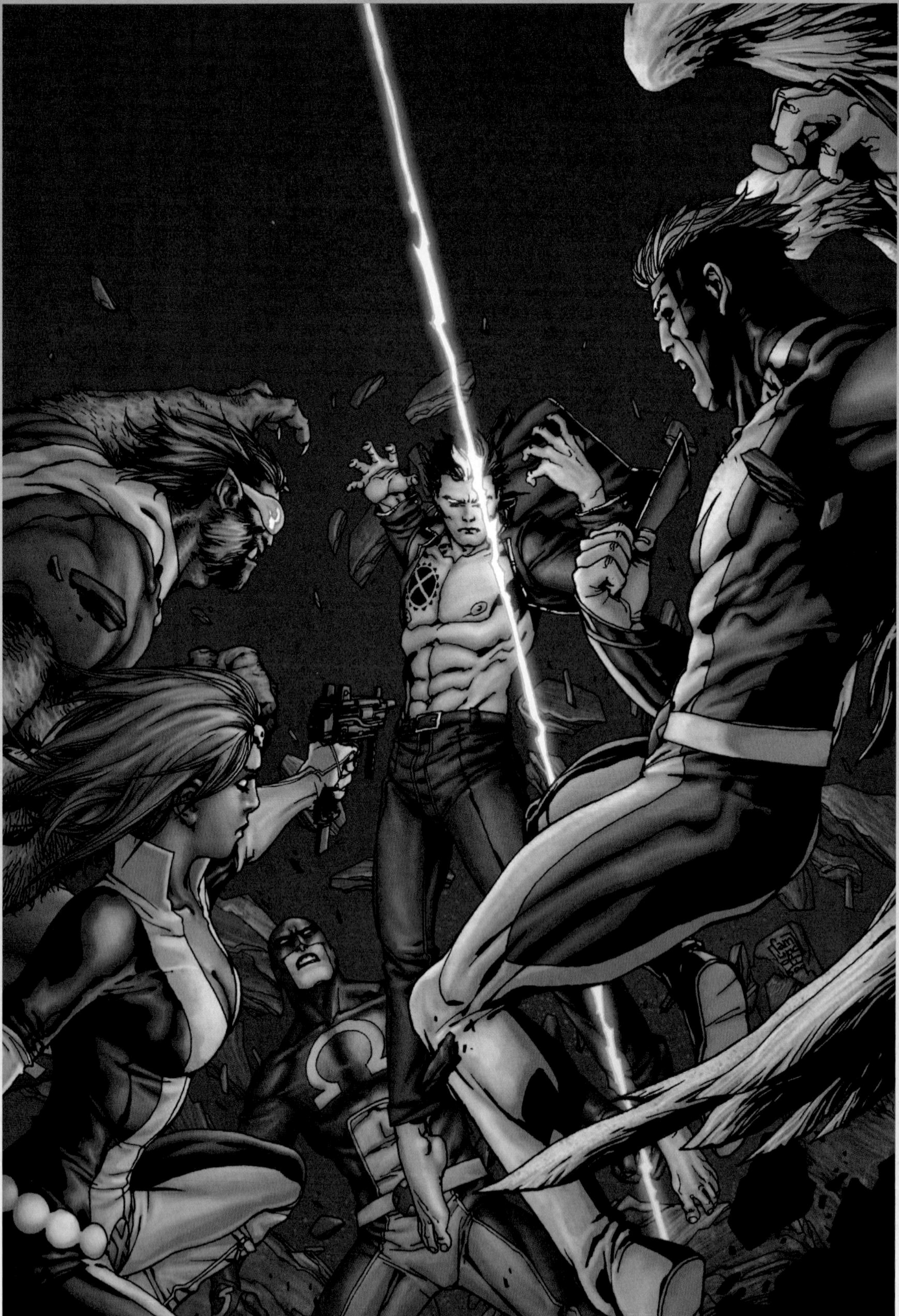

5

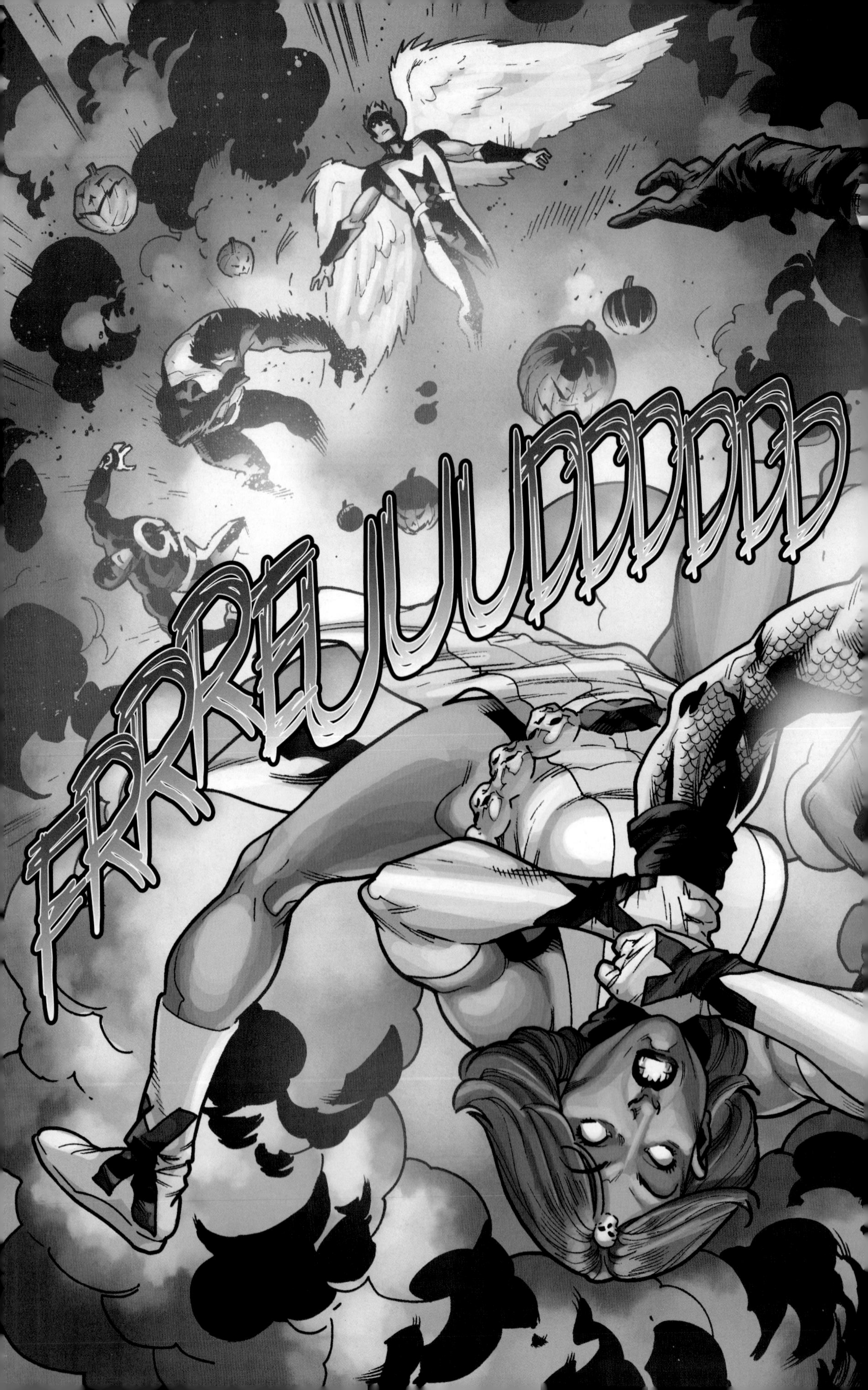
FRREUUUDDDDDDD

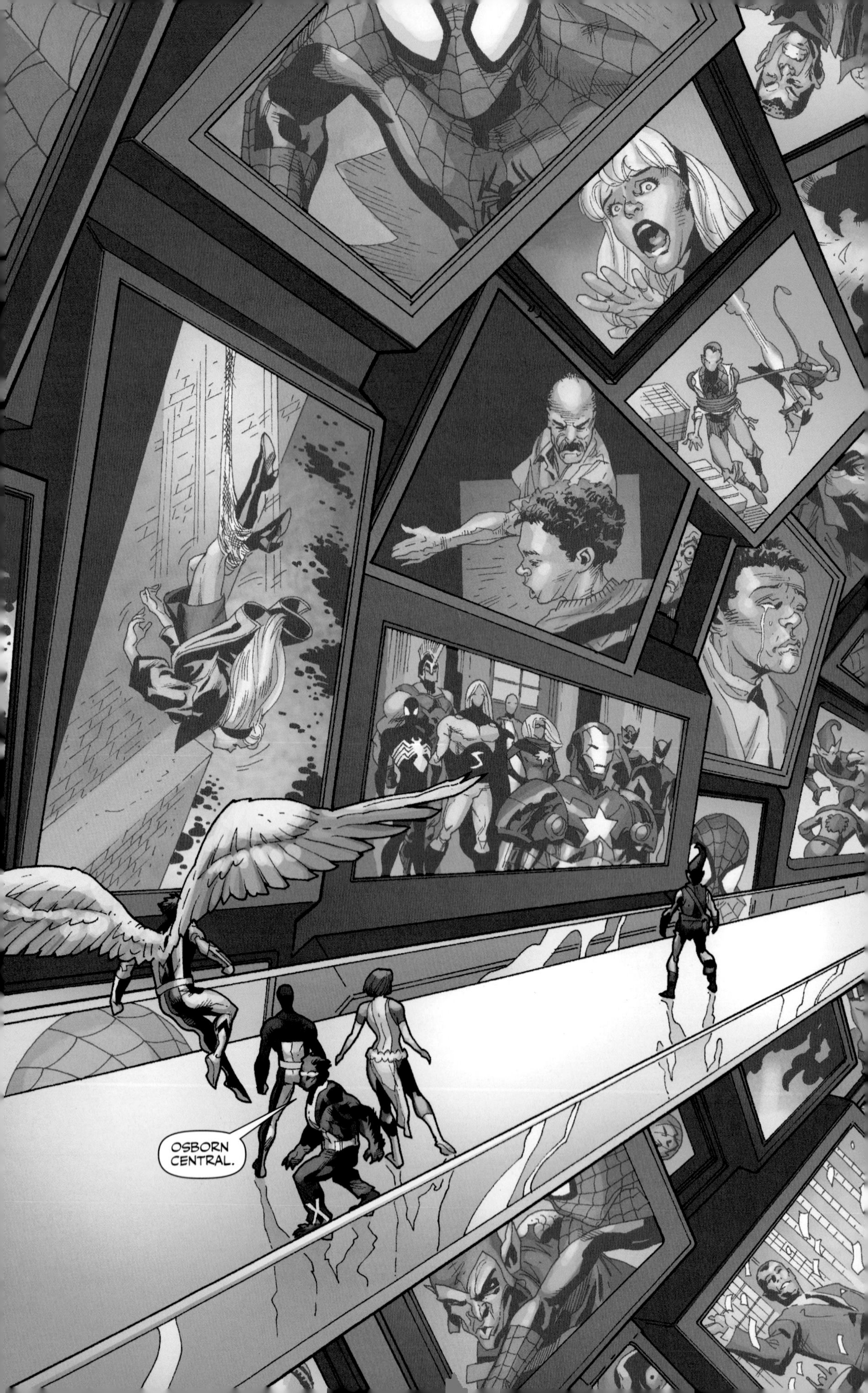
OSBORN CENTRAL.

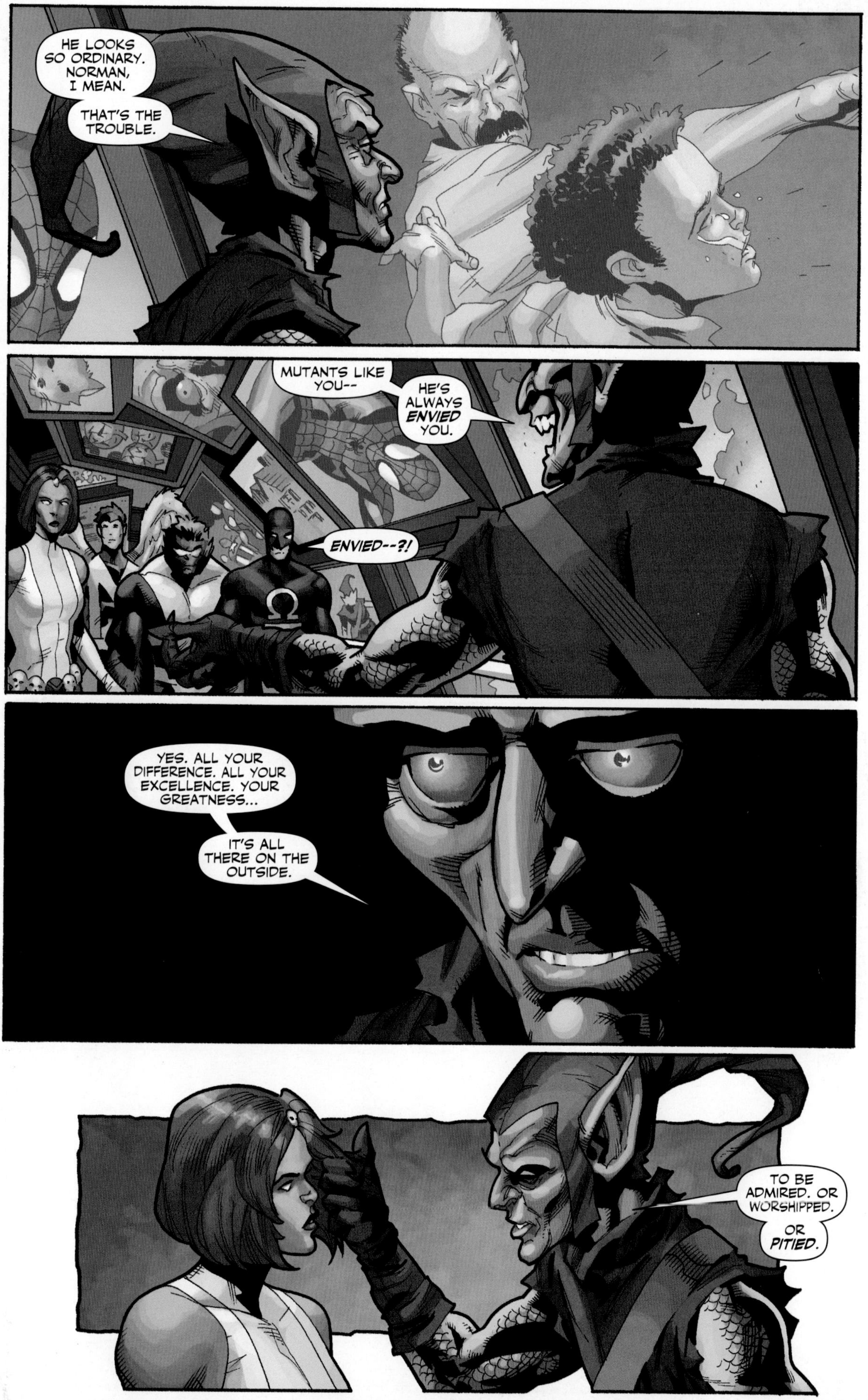

HE LOOKS SO ORDINARY. NORMAN, I MEAN.
THAT'S THE TROUBLE.
MUTANTS LIKE YOU--
HE'S ALWAYS *ENVIED* YOU.
ENVIED--?!
YES. ALL YOUR DIFFERENCE. ALL YOUR EXCELLENCE. YOUR GREATNESS...
IT'S ALL THERE ON THE OUTSIDE.
TO BE ADMIRED. OR WORSHIPPED.
OR *PITIED*.

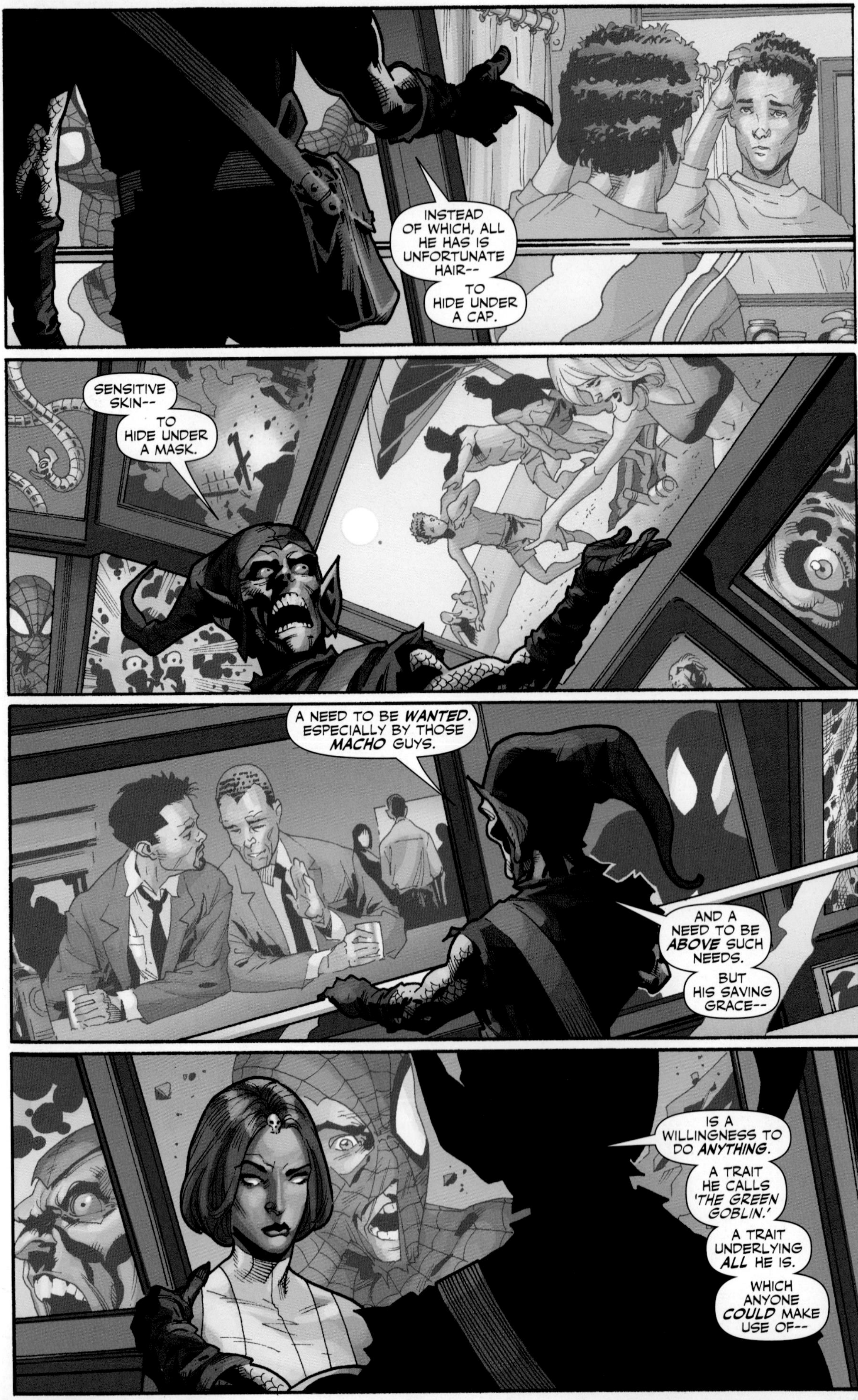
INSTEAD OF WHICH, ALL HE HAS IS UNFORTUNATE HAIR--
TO HIDE UNDER A CAP.
SENSITIVE SKIN--
TO HIDE UNDER A MASK.
A NEED TO BE *WANTED*. ESPECIALLY BY THOSE *MACHO* GUYS.
AND A NEED TO BE *ABOVE* SUCH NEEDS.
BUT HIS SAVING GRACE--
IS A WILLINGNESS TO DO *ANYTHING*.
A TRAIT HE CALLS *'THE GREEN GOBLIN.'*
A TRAIT UNDERLYING *ALL* HE IS.
WHICH ANYONE *COULD* MAKE USE OF--

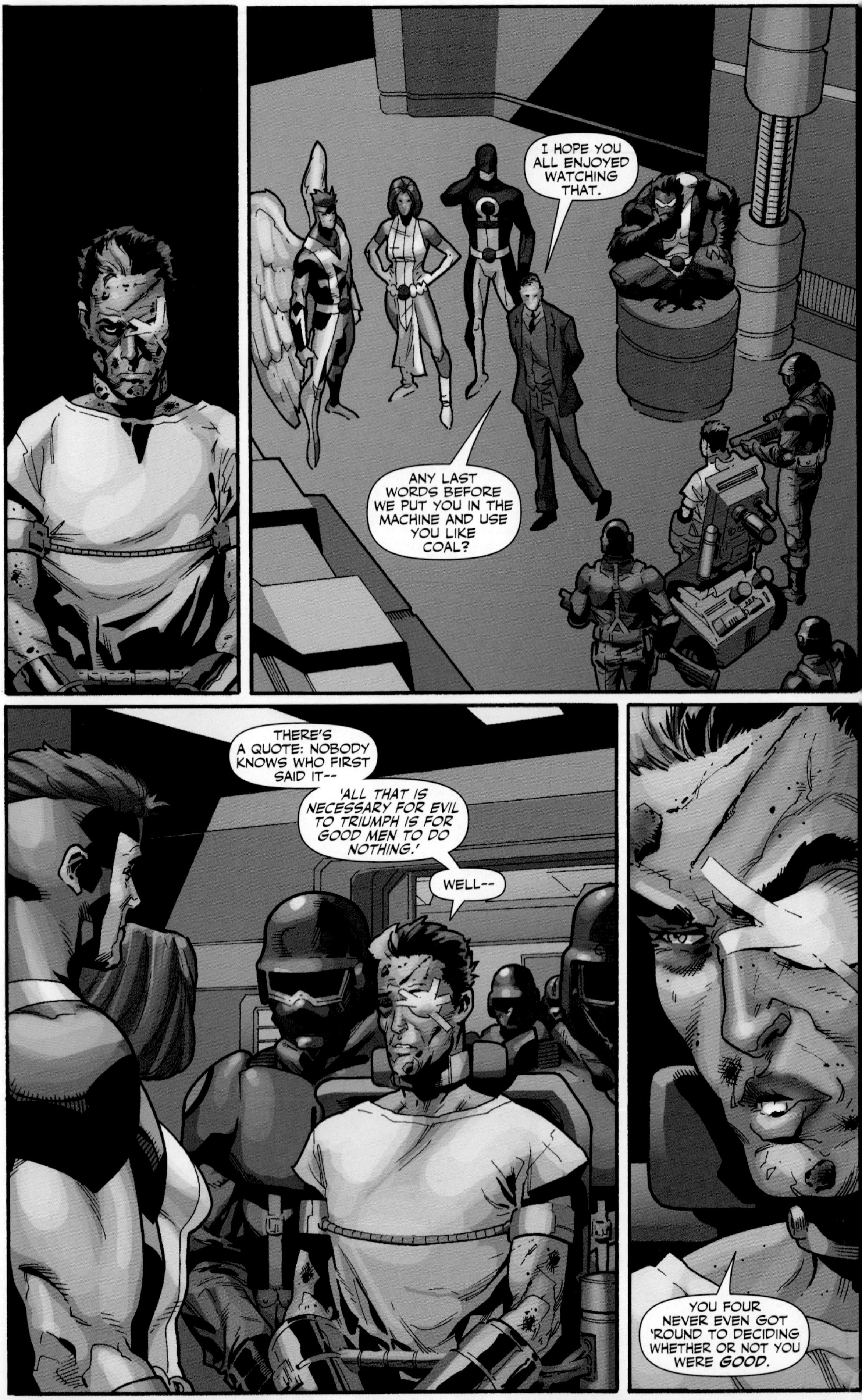
I HOPE YOU ALL ENJOYED WATCHING THAT.
ANY LAST WORDS BEFORE WE PUT YOU IN THE MACHINE AND USE YOU LIKE COAL?
THERE'S A QUOTE: NOBODY KNOWS WHO FIRST SAID IT--
'ALL THAT IS NECESSARY FOR EVIL TO TRIUMPH IS FOR GOOD MEN TO DO NOTHING.'
WELL--
YOU FOUR NEVER EVEN GOT 'ROUND TO DECIDING WHETHER OR NOT YOU WERE GOOD.

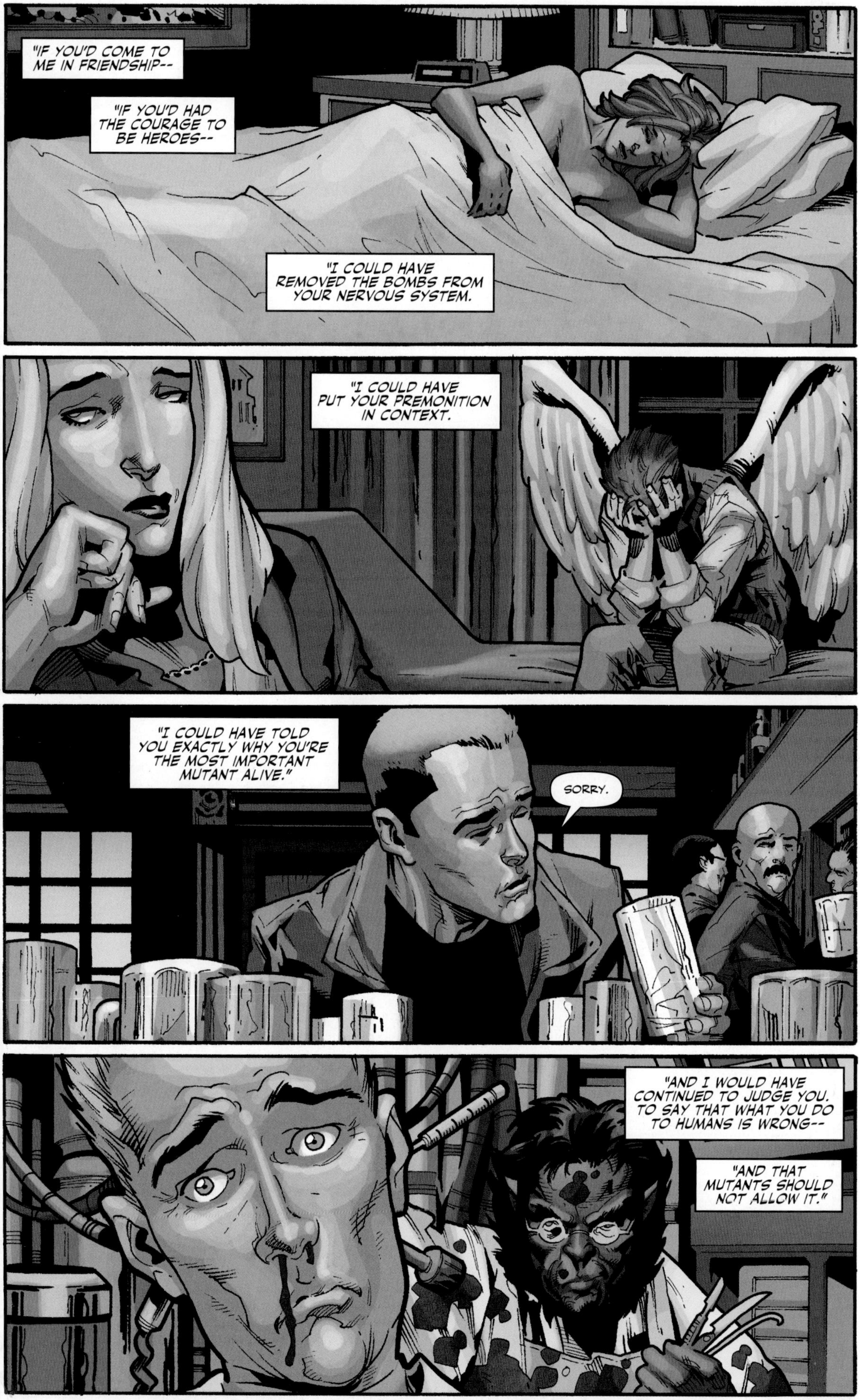
"IF YOU'D COME TO ME IN FRIENDSHIP--
"IF YOU'D HAD THE COURAGE TO BE HEROES--
"I COULD HAVE REMOVED THE BOMBS FROM YOUR NERVOUS SYSTEM.
"I COULD HAVE PUT YOUR PREMONITION IN CONTEXT.
"I COULD HAVE TOLD YOU EXACTLY WHY YOU'RE THE MOST IMPORTANT MUTANT ALIVE."
SORRY.
"AND I WOULD HAVE CONTINUED TO JUDGE YOU. TO SAY THAT WHAT YOU DO TO HUMANS IS WRONG--
"AND THAT MUTANTS SHOULD NOT ALLOW IT."

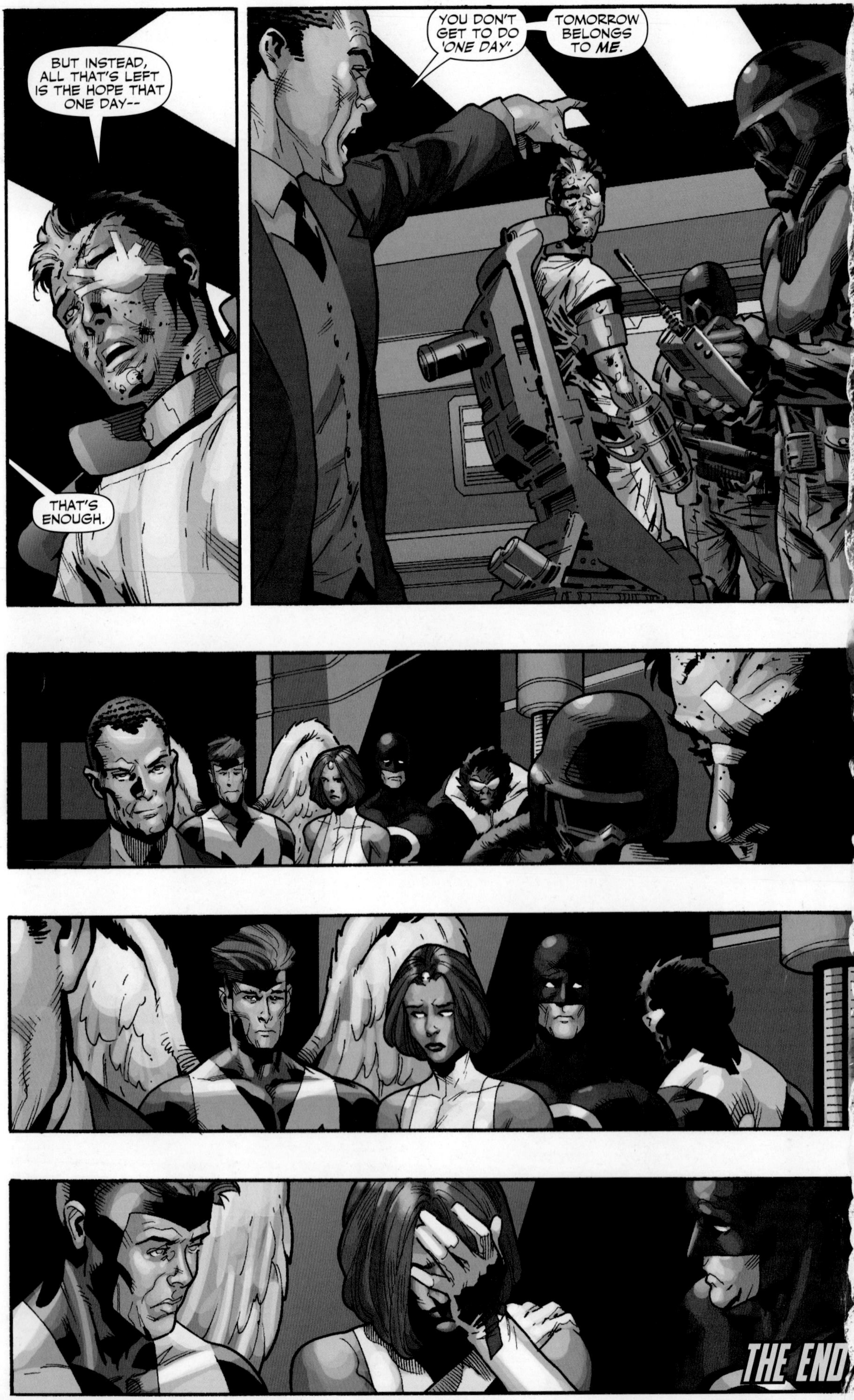
BUT INSTEAD, ALL THAT'S LEFT IS THE HOPE THAT ONE DAY--
THAT'S ENOUGH.
YOU DON'T GET TO DO 'ONE DAY'.
TOMORROW BELONGS TO ME.
THE END